terrors of the screen

by Frank Manchel

Illustrated with photographs

PRENTICE-HALL, INC., Englewood Cliffs, N.J.

To Grandma Ida

contents

IN THE EARLY DAYS

This book is about the special terrors that film-makers create, from the earliest days of crude theatrical tricks to the current emphasis on brutality, sex and violence. We shall explore a variety of motion pictures bringing us in contact with the strange, unbelievable world of fiends, monsters, vampires, phantoms, ghosts, witches, werewolves and the living dead. Each film, with its unique treatment and story, will contribute to our overall understanding of why so many people are so fascinated with terror films.

But the history of the world's fascination with macabre stories goes back many centuries before pictures began to move. It may well start at the point where primitive people huddled around their campfires to listen to strange tales told by men who had dared to go beyond the confines of the encampment. Seated there in the darkness of night, silhouetted against the leaping flames, they stared as bold warriors costumed and masked in the skins of dangerous animals danced and chanted about their terrifying adventures. Just as terror films of today, those haunting plays of

1

long ago taught the young about survival, stressed specific cultural values and celebrated special events. And just as we do now, the audiences then, curious and awestricken, watched in fear and gazed in amazement as exciting exploits took place before their eyes.

As man's curiosity with the unknown progressed over the centuries, so did his ability to tell his tales of terror. In ancient Greece, thousands of years ago, great playwrights wrote about fantastic heroes and heroines who faced incredible and horrifying experiences. But in those plays, terror took on a new and significant function—that of helping audiences to relieve their tensions and anxieties (or what the ancients called a catharsis). Thus ages ago enlightened men had sensed, as some critics of terror films today fail to understand, that the experience of seeing someone else's fears and troubles may help us to better face our own problems.

These brilliant dramatists also sensed that the most terrifying experience of all is what we ourselves imagine, and not what is shown on the stage by the use of special effects or costumes. As a result, the ancient Greeks stressed the importance of suggestion and implication in their suspenseful and terrifying dramas. In almost every play, the action moved carefully but slowly to the most horrifying moments, emphasizing how unsuspecting men and women could develop a false sense of security. And, at the moment when most people were unprepared, horror and terror struck, suddenly and swiftly. This excellent formula still works well with today's audiences.

In the generations that followed, creative men continued to explore a variety of imaginative ways to satisfy man's thirst for violence, excitement and terror. Then with the emergence of the novel and the short story, a new school of terror was created: the Gothic tale. Usually the events described took place in a fictitious medieval setting, filled with strange, mysterious and horrible incidents, in a terrifying atmosphere of darkness and fear. Anything was possible:

2

people were maimed, mutilated or buried alive only to return to torment their enemies, while strange sounds, billowing curtains and unexplainable disappearances terrorized the countryside. Every castle, manor house or home had a complete set of long, underground passageways, trap-doors, sliding panels and torture chambers. Thus H.G. Wells' Dr. Moreau conducted his work in secret, on a deserted patch of land, away from the eyes of his fellowman. Robert Louis Stevenson's Dr. Jekyll locked himself in his secret laboratory and then emerged through a special door as Mr. Hyde to walk down the dark, mysterious London streets. And Mary Shelley's young medical student found the forbidden materials for his unnatural experiments among the graves of the dead, in the lonely cemeteries and at the expense of his own life.

By the time moving pictures appeared at the end of the nineteenth century, mankind's irrepressible fascination with terror, dread and anxiety had been well landscaped. The screen had only to discover and develop its unique talents for shocking and terrorizing the audience.

What are some of these special abilities that the cinema possesses for depicting the horrific? Certainly one piece of evidence is the selective director's ability to control what we see and hear on the screen. Consider, for example, the classic terror scene we've seen in dozens of movies where the frightened woman is alone in her bedroom. By cleverly using strange noises on his sound track, the director suggests that there is someone or something in the hall. Next we hear nothing, and the clever film-maker begins to play on our imagination by the suspenseful pace in which he shifts from sounds to silence to sounds. The camera, too, shifts from shots of the woman sitting motionlessly in the darkness, not daring to make a noise, to close-up shots of the doorknob, at first in a fixed position. Then we see it begin to turn. By now, even the bravest of us begins to feel a little uncomfortable about what is going to happen next. And depending upon what the director wants us to feel, the thing turning the doorknob could be either a deadly creature or only a familiar character offering us a momentary scare. In fact, by selecting every major image for the audience, how and under what conditions the action occurs, using a specific pace and sound track, the inventive movie-maker can make us shudder in the presence of any man, woman, child or thing!

Another distinctive advantage for the director is trick photography, which takes us into the domain of skillfully constructed scale models, superbly developed film-laboratory processes, imaginatively conceived make-up and costuming, plus a host of outstanding motion picture technicians. When done well, special effects photography can create some of the most memorable visual experiences film-goers will ever have: the transformation of man to beast, the destruction of cities by earthquake, fire and flood, and the collision of worlds. So vivid and exciting are these scenes that many in the audience hide in their seats, too frightened to sit upright until the terror has passed.

Probably most impressive of all is the cinema's gift of hypnotizing us into a dreamlike trance that captures our feelings and moods as well as our thoughts. Sitting in a darkened auditorium, looking up at those giant, strange shapes that move, each of us is mesmerized by the overwhelming dramatic presence of terror.

It is not surprising, therefore, that the first man to explore the screen's fantastic potential for depicting terror was a professional magician whose roots were in the theatrical tradition of stage illusions, at a time when the theater had become the last refuge for monsters, conjurers and delusions.

George Méliès—sometimes referred to as the King of the Fantasmagoria, the Jules Verne of the Cinema, the Magician of the Screen—gave up the ownership of a magic sideshow at thirty-four, shortly after watching a special performance of the Lumière Brothers' revolutionary invention, a motion picture projector which they called the cinematographe. Although the Lumières failed to appreciate the significance of their toy, Méliès realized its power to mystify. Unable to convince the inventors of his theory, the amiable Frenchman set out on his own to make his fortune with moving pictures.

With an avowed purpose to perplex and startle people, Méliès purchased some equipment and began making movies in his backyard. But more often than not, the weather worked against him. Obviously what he needed was a conservatory of his own where he could control the elements. By the end of 1897, Méliès had built at Montreuil, France, a Paris suburb, the first film studio in the world that boasted glass walls and a glass ceiling, a movable stage, and a remarkable assortment of theatrical facilities, including such basic trick operations as trap doors and scrim curtains. Actually, the studio very much resembled a theater, and everything that occurred in Méliès' movies, seen as though actually being performed on a stage, mirrored the long theatrical history of magic, mystery and make-believe.

Performers made their entrances and exits in the traditional stage manner, while the camera, stationed in a medium-long shot position of the theater audience, recorded the action from the point of view of the ticket holder seated in the front row.

By testing artificial lighting, various cameras and rolls of film, Méliès quickly developed or refined a number of widely accepted techniques now quite common in motion picture production. One was the fade-out or -in, which created the impression that the picture was either disappearing or just coming into focus. Another improvement was the over-lap dissolve. This time he used one shot merging into another one to create the illusion of change from one image to another. He also created some marvelous ghostlike effects by shooting the same shot twice, each time using a different lighting exposure known as the double exposure shot. Probably best of all was his stop motion photography experiments where he would film the action up to a certain point, then stop the shooting, and after substituting a key object in the shot, begin shooting the scene at the precise moment he had stopped. When the movie was projected, the audience thought it saw a miracle occur as objects mysteriously vanished before their eyes. In experiments such as these, the inventive Frenchman found that by using a black velvet backdrop he could easily make several exposures of the same shot without destroying the audience's impression of seeing the action actually occur in one continuous scene. Combining his photographic skill with careful planning and execution of prepared scenarios, using theatrically staged scenes as a trademark and filming handsomely costumed players against ornate backgrounds, the master magician continued to startle and mystify his patrons. Some of his most popular successes were appropriately entitled *The Vanishing Lady, The Haunted Castle, A Nightmare,* and *The Conjurer.*

No one was his rival in those primitive years. By 1902, he had made well over 350 movies mostly devoted to illusions, surprises and tricks. In two-minute reels, one after another, actors miraculously vanished, mysteriously flew through the air, suddenly were transformed into animals, got sawed in half and then put back together, rocketed to the moon and returned. Everyone spoke of his work, and his methods were imitated everywhere.

Then, in 1903, six short years after he had begun, Méliès' popularity began to wane. New advances were being made that pointed out inherent weaknesses in his techniques so much so that the Frenchman's films became a source of amusement rather than of fear. No satisfactory reason has been given why he did not make use of the new developments, but the fact remains that he did not. Here and there, he produced an unusual or charming film, but for all outward purposes, no one noticed when a combination of poor business practices and the advent of World War I forced Méliès to stop film production in 1913. Further duress caused this marvelous man—who many claimed remained a child throughout his life—to sell his studio and theater in 1925. By then bitter, lonely and broke, he burned most of his available prints, thereby depriving future generations of watching many of those imaginative moving pictures that so startled the earliest of film-goers. Although he died in 1938, poor in material wealth, Méliès has earned the respect of every major artist working in the motion picture industry.

Méliès was not unique in his close cinematic ties with the theater and the literary classics. By 1912, most major film companies recognized the advantages of translating tales from the traditional arts to the screen: prestige, popularity and, mainly, profit. Before turning our attention to some of the important terror films of the silent era, we might better appreciate the artists if we had some idea of what production conditions were like, particularly in the movie center of the world—the United States.

To say that film-making was informal from 1900 to 1915 is a gross understatement. A classic example is William Fox's scenario department where most of his early movies originated in the mind of his wife. Mrs. Fox either told him stories in the evening as they drove home from work, or in the morning before he left for the studio. By the end of the day, minor changes had been made in the plot, players had been recruited, sets located, and technicians rounded up. By the end of the week, again with the help of his wife, who also wrote the subtitles, Mr. Fox was producing, distributing and exhibiting a number of new motion pictures.

Or take the example of Thanhouser Studios, which inserted a Siberian scene in one of their moving pictures because an unexpected snowfall had buried their building. The snow did not remain long enough to complete the film, so the audience read an ingenious subtitle: "Later—A Warmer Clime."

Obviously, if the movies were going to achieve any status as an important art form, changes had to be made.

One necessary prerequisite to artistic films was an improved lighting system. In these early times, lighting was considered synonymous with illumination; all that mattered was that there be enough light to photograph the players. Few people in the motion picture industry sensed the significance of controlled, diffused and reflected light for enhancing the visual and dramatic qualities of a movie.

Another necessary prerequisite was the camera itself. In order to make the photographic box more mobile and manageable, its size, shape and weight had to be altered. More often than not, the usual practice was to place the awkward machine in a stationary position, have the shot lined up and focused, and then instruct the performers to play their parts in a carefully defined and limited area. Although talented men like Billy Bitzer and D.W. Griffith had by 1912 developed most of the fundamental features of a screen grammar, few producers felt obligated to change their shooting methods.

Film makers were also considerably hampered by the poor quality and limited possibility of the available film stock. Because orthochromatic film reacted unevenly and unpredictably to the color spectrum, particularly red, the shooting results often proved disasterous as well as disappointing. Consequently, experimentation was discouraged and the art of composing a shot remained relatively unknown.

Understandably, no formula for picturing terror existed at this time. But producers were beginning to try and test the commercial possibilities. Thomas Alva Edison, for instance, released a *Frankenstein* movie including, in one critic's opinion, a "quite fearsome" monster. Edison, also distributed a thriller of sorts entitled *Sherlock Holmes and the Giant Murder*, a two-for-one literary adaption of Arthur Conan Doyle and Edgar Allan Poe. In addition, other film companies offered one-reel science-fiction chills (such as *The Wizard*, featuring an obnoxious ape-man), a growing assortment of "exciting and death-defying" serials (like the unbelievable chapters of *The Perils of Pauline*, where the stars experienced more danger in making the serials than the audience witnessed in the chapters themselves), and screen translations of popular mystery plays (particularly the 1908 Selig production of *Dr. Jekyll and Mr. Hyde,* in which the Chicago firm paid a road company of actors to perform onstage while the cameraman filmed the story from the audience).

To a great degree, the problems inherent in making terror films were illustrated by the close connection between the traditional arts and the art of the' film. No clearer example for our purposes exists than the Thanhouser Studio's 1912 production of Robert Louis Stevenson's *The Strange Case of Dr. Jekyll and Mr. Hyde,* the source for the stage play that had been filmed earlier. In this most enduring and popular of Stevenson's stories, admittedly sentimental and contrived, the author's magnificent literary qualities and his intriguing discussion of man's complex personality elevated the novella into an excellent vehicle for dramatic presentations of schizophrenia.

Thanhouser was typical of most of the early studios. It placed a maximum effort on the profit aspect of the industry and a minimum concern on the artistic development of film. But the two efforts were beginning to merge by this time and the trend was to collect talented people, to develop a kind of human stable where performers could remain minor but familiar trademarks of a particular studio. Two of Thanhouser's family were Marguerite Snow, well-known for her delightful performance of the gypsy temptress, Carmen, and her husband, James Cruze, soon to become one of Hollywood's most famous directors.

Lucius Henderson directed these two artists in a one-reel version of the Stevenson story, by now the third try at portraying the Victorian version of good and evil in man, The Great Northern Company of Copenhagen had made the second film (six in all would be screened before the end of the silent era, establishing it as one of the most fashionable of all types to make). Henderson's film promised more than it delivered. In James Cruze he had a competent actor whose theatrical skills allowed him to play the dual role of the reserved inquisitive scientist and the grotesque, active fiend. In spite of the fixed and unchanging position of the camera, the same consistent and thus meaningless lighting, and the impoverished set, Cruze created the slow-moving existence of the individual who secretly tested his theory that certain drugs could separate a man into two beings—one good and the other bad. The opening shots hurriedly moved us from establishing the situation to the determined man's private laboratory, and then Henderson slowed down the pace of the film considerably by having Cruze take an incredible amount of screen time to prepare both the formula and the antidote. Particularly interesting was the director's framing or photographing of the action in the laboratory. Dr. Jekyll is positioned for most of this scene at screen right, thereby not only confining his movement but also emphasizing the slowness of the individual. The effect works wonderfully, providing us with a visual contrast between the static qualities of the good doctor and the hyperactivities of the evil Hyde, who leaps about the screen like a caged animal. Although the man's transformation, after drinking the formula, into a fiend with protruding teeth is crudely handled—in one instance a single frame separates the white-haired scientist from the dark-haired villain—Cruze's skill at pantomime overcomes the missing and necessary help that film actors expect from editing, camera work, set design and lighting conditions.

But there the credits end. The plot plods on, the actions become absurd and repetitive, and the end comes mercifully a short time later. No one seemed to know what to show, when to stop, or how to terrorize.

Then in the years following World War I, one nation came to grips with the problem, and the beginning of the great terror films arrived.

10

Although this type of artificially arranged scene from Méliès' film *Conquest of the Pole* (1912) did little to advance the art of the film, it does indicate the influence of the theater on the early film-makers.

(THE BETTMANN ARCHIVE, INC.)

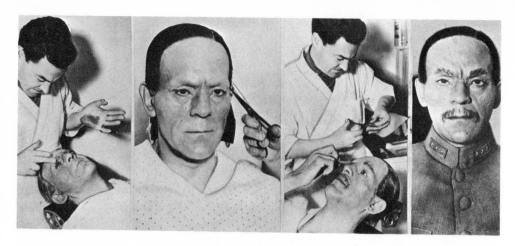

Boris Karloff being made-up by Jack Pierce. During the first few years of the 1930's, these men created two of the most memorable movie monsters of all time: Frankenstein's creature and the mummy.

(THE BETTMANN ARCHIVE, INC.)

In this shot from Méliès' 1902 masterpiece *A Trip to the Moon,* we have an example of his mixture of humor, special effects, and shock.

(HERMAN G. WEINBERG COLLECTION)

In the screen version of H.G. Wells' *The Island of Lost Souls* (1932) Charles Laughton appeared as Dr. Moreau who turned animals into men. Here we see the unfortunate surgeon and his angry patients.

(BETTMANN/SPRINGER FILM ARCHIVE)

Spencer Tracy in *Dr. Jekyll and Mr. Hyde* (1941). Compare this laboratory scene with the one in *The Werewolf of London*. Notice how shadow and light play a crucial role in establishing atmosphere.

(THE BETTMANN ARCHIVE, INC.)

John Barrymore as Mr. Hyde in *Dr. Jekyll and Mr. Hyde* (1920).
(HERMAN G. WEINBERG COLLECTION)

No tale of terror has more frequently been performed on the screen than Robert Louis Stevenson's *Dr. Jekyll and Mr. Hyde.* Here we have Fredric March in his 1932 academy award role as both Dr. Jekyll and Mr. Hyde.

FROM SOUL TO SCREEN

The aftermath of World War I conflict dramatically transformed the controversial status of the terror film from that of an insignificant one-reeler to a feature film of considerable importance, primarily because of the war's commercial, artistic, and social effects on the German cinema. Here in the ravaged country of strange legends and foreboding myths, film intellectuals began the first serious examination of screen terror.

Actually the Teutonic interest in the fantastic harmonized with the internationally renowned German theater, then under the remarkable guidance of producer-director Max Reinhardt. Probably more than any other individual at this moment in film history, he provided the essential preparation for terror on celluloid. Of utmost importance for future motion picture productions was his creative revolution away from ornate and static stagecraft and toward a simplified but artistically created set coupled with breathtaking lighting effects. The primary emphasis was on presenting an expressive, imaginative point of view rather than an actual facsimile of life. The actors, directors and technicians who studied first with Reinhardt and then were absorbed into the movie industry took with them precisely these skills of expressive craftsmanship, psychological overtones, and simplicity of storytelling that made his stage so prominent in the intellectual life of the German people.

These professional and recognized artists also brought a new respectability to the emerging art form, which up to 1910 was considered a cheap escape for the unemployed, the uneducated, and the unimportant. Now that the intellectual élite were becoming involved in movie aesthetics, former film audiences accustomed to superficial plots and crude performances were surprised at the strangeness of the images and the seriousness of the stories.

Paul Wegener became one of the first of the Reinhardt disciples to enter the cinematic world. In many respects he resembled Méliès: He drew upon a rich theatrical background, became fascinated with the potential of the screen for depicting the fantastic, and proved to be an extremely innovative artist. But here the similarities end. The happy-go-lucky magician of Montreuil never delved very deeply into the fiendish aspects of life that so troubled this imaginative German star.

Wegener's initial screen performance was in the 1913 terror film *The Student of Prague,* the forerunner of many meaningful movie treatments of ancient legends. The plot, suggested by the famous Faust stories, E.T.A. Hoffman, and Edgar Allan Poe, focused on an impoverished student, Baldwin, whose desperate search for love and wealth results in an eerie meeting in his pitiful attic with the evil wizard Scapinelli, actually an earthly representation of the devil. A contract is signed by the two, stating that if the sorcerer provided him with a suitable mate, the student would relinquish all rights to his reflected mirror image. At the outset things go well for Baldwin. Although his intended bride has an outraged lover who challenges the young man to a duel, Baldwin is clearly the superior fencer. He secretly promises his future father-in-law to spare the suitor's life and expects the entire affair to enhance his position with the family. Then Scapinelli interferes. Delaying Baldwin on some meaningless pretext, the sinister spirit (in what several critics claim was a remarkable cinematic achievement for its day) draws the reflected image from the mirror and transforms it into a lifelike double of the student, who then substitutes for Baldwin at the duel and kills his rival. Unable to convince anyone of the trick, disgraced and dishonored, Baldwin returns to the scene of the compact and in a fit of vengeance shoots his false image, thereby unwittingly killing himself. The film ends with Scapinelli claiming not only the corpse, but probably the soul as well.

The value of *The Student of Prague* (remade after World War I) transcended the film itself. In some respects it highlighted the effect that Swedish and Danish movies were having on German studios, particularly the emphasis on character studies of past eras, serious themes and impressive productions. Also valuable were the interpretations of various psychological obsessions suggested by the screen performances as well as the increased use of trick photography for narrative motion pictures. Most important, the role of Baldwin provided the star with fresh material for another bizarre screenplay.

It seems that while the film company was in Prague to record some exterior shots, Wegener, a lifelong student of myths, fairytales and legends, came across the medieval story of Rabbi Judah Lowe Ben Bezalel, who, in order to prevent the Jewish people from being massacred by a threatened pogrom, created from clay a legendary robot, the Golem, whose noble purpose was to protect the oppressed Jews. Intrigued by the theme and by the persistent rumors in the city itself that such an incident had actually occurred in history, Wegener decided to make a motion picture based upon this bit of Talmudic lore. (Before finishing his screen career, the serious artist made three versions of the legend.)

Wegener released his second terror picture, *The Golem*, early in 1915, sharing the directing credits with screenwriter, Henrik Galeen, whose intense interest in preparing a visual script elevated the craft of screenwriting to new heights. (That stories lent themselves to visual effects soon became the overriding concern of film makers.) The legend itself became modernized: laborers digging for a well on the site of an ancient synagogue discover a clay statue, which they quickly sell to an antique dealer. Learning both the value of the newly acquired property and the means by which it can be brought back to life, the antiquarian brings the Golem magically back into being for the sole purpose of satisfying the selfish collector's personal needs. But once alive, the pitiful creature falls madly in love with the man's daughter, whose obvious horror of his monstrous form drives him to complete despair. Desperately trying to win her affections, the frustrated Golem savagely destroys everything in his way and in the end only his shattering fall from a lofty tower saves the populace.

Once again Wegener drew upon his former training with Reinhardt, producing a motion picture which tried, not altogether successfully, to integrate make-up, special effects, an intelligent but simple script, a well-designed setting and competent acting. Most noteworthy was the way he arranged his scenes into a series of sets, or what is known as a composite set, so that he could do his filming in chronological order.

Just as the first movie had suggested the second, so also did the themes of *The Golem* provide the basis for the third and most popular of the terror films of the war years: *Homunculus*, a six-chapter, six-hour serial about an artifically constructed monster, a creature "without a soul, the devil's servant."

The 1916 screenplay reiterated what had by now become the traditional terror story of man-made monsters: mad scientist creates super-human monster, monster falls in love with beautiful girl who rejects him, monster revenges himself on the world. Up until the final chapter, the man-made monster, now out of anyone's control, brings disaster on community after community, each time escaping the wrath of the people. Finally in chapter six, the demented creation is struck dead by a propitious and symbolic bolt of lightning, presumably from the heavens.

All three films underscored among other characteristics the dangers all of us face from abnormal experiments and sacrilegious interests, turning those who are denied fundamental human love into lustful monsters and Satan's unsuspecting accomplices. In each instance, death and destruction were directly attributed to psychologically disturbed individuals who were lonely, frustrated and misunderstood.

By late 1919, most of Germany's leading motion picture corporations were being underwritten with large sums of money from the Weimar Republic, which first saw in movies a meaningful way of restoring a dwindling national pride, and later recognized that the film industry provided the country with some excellent propaganda as well as a valuable economic product for world distribution.

Motivated more and more by financial needs, many important studios decided it was to their best interests to merge into one giant organization, which could then provide them with bigger, better and more elaborate production facilities. And so it was that the fabulous UFA, with its major studios at Neubabelsberg and Staaken, began the haunting but golden era of the cinema east of the Rhine.

These were the years where the 100 percent studio-made film characterized the work of Germany's greatest directors and technicians, where the stress was placed upon the unique cinematic effects that could be achieved by dramatic visual composition and creatively designed architecture: a fantasy world of shadows, lights, flat canvases, and hanging drapes. It was an interest especially suited to the egos of the early motion picture artists. They too wanted recognition from the larger world of the established arts where since 1911 the intellectual emphasis was on replacing stores and pictures of what we actually see with drama and images of what we feel, an expressionist *outlook on experience*. The movement itself clearly mirrored the difficulties of a war-ravaged country where the distraught Germans were in a never-ending struggle for the basic necessities of life.

Then one autumn day in 1919, there came to Delca Studios and to its visionary producer Erich Pommer two disenchanted young screenwriters, Hans Janowitz and Carl Mayer, who submitted an original story, *The Cabinet of Dr. Caligari*. The film, the producer, the stars, and the scenarists were all to play a conspicuous role in the history of motion pictures from then on.

The idea for the script originated first with Janowitz. During a visit to the 1913 Hamburg fair, he became distracted by the strange behavior of a mysterious middle-class man he saw lurking near some bushes in a park on the Holstenwall. After reading in the following morning's newspaper of an unsolved sex murder that had been committed in that exact location, Janowitz, out of curiosity, attended the slain girl's funeral, where he had the unexplainable feeling that he alone knew who the murderer was. The crime was never solved and Janowitz firmly believed that there were many such murderers loose in society, and nothing was being done to stop them. A few years later, after the war had ended, Janowitz met the Austrian poet Mayer and related his unusual experience. In turn, the disillusioned ex-German infantry officer, now an avowed pacifist, told Janowitz of his bitter examinations by a military psychiatrist who had malicously discounted the poet's beliefs as the thoughts of an unbalanced mind. The two decided to write a story and considered a variety of ways in which their painful experiences could be turned into a dramatic screenplay. The answer came, so folklore has it, late one evening when the two aspiring writers witnessed the performance of a small town magician of considerable strength who predicted fortunes. The name of their main character—Caligari—was selected by Mayer from a series of letters he had been reading by the French author Stendhal.

The story's setting is the small town of Holstenwall, where a travelling fair attracts the evil montebank, Dr. Caligari, and his hypnotized sleep-walker, Cesare, endowed with amazing fortune-telling powers. The mysterious showman, seeking permission from the town clerk to perform at the carnival, is granted a license only after being subjected to a number of indignities; the next day, the pompous official is found murdered. That same afternoon, two students, Alan and Francis, attending the sleepwalker's performance, hear Cesare foretell Alan's death at dawn. When the prophecy proves true, Francis suspects Caligari of foul play. His suspicions appear false when the police announce they have already arrested another man for the crimes. Yet the terror continues. This time Cesare, bent on murdering Francis' betrothed, Jane, finds the girl too lovely to harm; instead, he tries to kidnap her, but Jane's screams save her from the brute. Although he narrowly escapes the pursuing mob, Cesare collapses in the wilderness from exhaustion and dies from exposure. Realizing that he is in danger from the police, Caligari flees, unknowingly followed by Francis. The trail ends at a lunatic asylum where Caligari's true identity as director of the mental institution is revealed. The original screenplay ends with the insane official being placed in a straitjacket.

There is little doubt that the two authors intended their drama to present revolutionary ideas, to reveal authorities as demented people whose mad desire for power takes precedence over all ethical principles and human rights. Cesare, the mindless dupe, symbolized the average citizen whose blind acceptance of military discipline allowed him to kill without emotion. Caligari's real position identified the true villains of society as those exalted, respected authorities whose disguised lust for unlimited power had turned them into twisted and tormented tyrants. Francis, the hero of the narrative, represented Truth, who saw through the thinly veiled plans of these dangerous tyrants and exposed their threat to the country.

Much to the authors' surprise, Pommer immediately accepted the story and entrusted its production to one of his most promising directors, Fritz Lang. Before going very far with his new assignment, Lang was recalled to a previous film which he had not yet completed. He did, however, suggest two important considerations: first, change the emphasis of the plot from an attack on authority to a defense of it; and second, turn the film over to Dr. Robert Weine, who had already done some recent work for the studio. Both recommendations had telling effects on the outcome of the movie.

In spite of violent protests from the authors, the film begins with a shot of Francis sitting on a bench with an older man, who has just remarked that there are sinister spirits surrounding him. At that moment, Jane, dressed in a long white gown, beautiful but bewildered, walks past them, apparently in a trance. Francis explains that he and his betrothed have just gone through the most terrifying experience, and then starts to recount the strange tale, the original Caligari scenario. The end of the movie was also changed: it is the student, not Caligari who is committed, and we recognize that the two men have been sitting all along in the garden of the insane asylum. Soon we see Jane and Cesare with other disturbed inmates and Francis being forcibly restrained, with a closing shot of the director supposedly grasping the cause of the young man's illness.

Obviously, this framing device, which was soon to become one of the most familiar conventions in motion pictures, completely reversed the revolutionary thrust of the original idea; the theme now stressed that we who dare question authority are the insane ones, and that society needs to be protected from us.

There were also other intriguing developments connected with this significant film. Janowitz wanted an experimental painter to design the sets, but Weine chose instead three contemporary artists, one of whose stated aims was to make motion pictures which were "drawings brought to life." Legend has it that when these modern artists began work at the studio, they discovered that Delca's electrical and power supply was severely limited by the rationing regulations of the post-war period. To offset the anticipated illumination problems of filming, the artists painted onto the flat canvases the desired black and white lighting effects that the shooting script recommended. At first, Pommer expressed considerable doubt about the advisability of combining modern art with actual people, but he was soon won over. The finished sets were a startling series of photographed paintings: emotional portraits of an unhealthy society with dark, brooding architecture, strange combinations of shadows, jagged lines and cryptic signs; an artist's interpretation of a reality which for him symbolized the weird thoughts of a diseased mind.

In many of the key roles Pommer cast former Reinhardt students, most of whom became stars of the world screen: Werner Krauss (Caligari), Conrad Veidt (Cesare), Friedrich Feher (Francis), and Lil Dagover (Jane). Each performer provided the viewer with a controversial but memorable interpretation of a macabre, morbid and mindless hallucination.

24

Equally controversial and memorable were the special lighting effects which suggested more than they showed, particularly, the murder of Alan through shadows cast on his bedroom wall; the ingenious props of high stools and giant desks which symbolized the supposed arrogance of the police and the town clerk; the stage directions which had Alan, as the excited student, coaxing Francis to go to the fair and pulling him into Caligari's side-show; and the marvelous pictorial composition which began almost every shot of the carnival with an organ grinder operating his machine against the background of an endlessly whirling merry-go-round, suggestive of a chaotic society.

Dr. Siegfried Kracauer, to whom every film historian owes an immeasurable debt of gratitude for his work on the German cinema, described the stereotyped characterizations, the symbolic settings and the stylized mannerisms as a kind of street sign, whose words were to be understood as "Soul at Work."

By 1920, when *The Cabinet of Dr. Caligari* was released and causing a sensation all over the artistic world with its electrifying techniques and story, the major conventions of the terror film were almost complete: the insane scientists, the pathetic but nevertheless terrifying monsters, the living dead who at first follow the blind dictates of their twisted masters and then revolt, the courageous young men who brave death for their loves, and the helpless heroines forever in danger from demonic and lustful adversaries. In this same year, Galeen and Wegener released a second and visually more-satisfying version of *The Golem*, while Janowitz translated *Dr. Jekyll and Mr. Hyde* to the German screen with Conrad Veidt in the demanding dual role.

The director of the new Stevenson picture was Friedrich Wilhelm Murnau, a former Reinhardt actor now turned cinematic genius. Of all the men, then and now, who have worked in the make-believe world of moving pictures, Murnau might well be one of the greatest. Few, if any, have ever surpassed his ability to sustain a mood by the use of shots alone, the imagination he demonstrated in freeing the camera from the fixed position it had maintained since the first days of film, and the tightness in editing that distingushed most of his movies.

Murnau fitted in very nicely with the somber, brooding era of haunting film production, probably because he shared the current fascination for combining the controversial values of experimental artists with the traditional terrifying pleasure of Gothic romances. It was not surprising, therefore, when news leaked out that Galeen and Murnau were working on a screenplay dealing with the most horrible yet most popular of all nefarious creatures: the vampire, the being who belongs neither to this world nor to the next.

Owing to copyright laws, the scenario, which was based upon the classic Bram Stoker Gothic novel of 1897 entitled *Dracula,* had to be loosely translated from its printed source. So the setting of the action takes place in Bremen, not London, during the plague year of 1838, not the late 1800's. The creature's name is Count Orlock, not Count Dracula, and the title is *Nosferatu (The Undead).*

The movie begins with a kind of deceptive prologue in the coastal town of Bremen, where Renfield, a real estate agent who is secretly under the power of the evil Count, dispatches his unsuspecting and newly married clerk to settle some business at the Count's castle. The apparent financial opportunities connected with the unusual assignment override any doubts the ambitious young man feels about departing from Nina, his wife. Once we leave the Baltic town, the by-now-familiar conventions of the terror film begin. Jonathan Harker's journey to Transylvania through the Carpathian woods and mountains, presents a wealth of visual horror motifs: a weird and remote corner of the globe where sinister animals prowl the earth, an ominous atmosphere of waste and barrenness pervades the landscape, and villagers, pale with fear, cross themselves as they recoil at the stranger's announced destination. Finally, one fateful night the trip is finished, and we encounter Count Orlock, a long-legged, bald, rat-faced host, more bones than flesh. After a strange meal and even stranger talk, Harker goes to bed. The next day, the worried clerk, finding some strange marks on the side of his throat and visibly shaken by the suspicious gossip he has heard from the townspeople, searches throughout the castle for his client. He eventually finds him in the cellar, stretched out in a coffin, corpse-like, with burning eyes wide-open; Harker in a perceptive instant of terror, realizes that he is a virtual prisoner of a vampire. Later that same night, Orlock, now safe from the dangerous daylight and seeking blood to sustain him, enters the sleeping victim's bedchamber. But Nina, hundreds of miles away, sensing her husband's peril, wakes from a feverish nightmare screaming her loved one's name and miraculously drives the vampire away from Harker. (This original incident was designed by Galeen to emphasize the power of love against the evil forces of the netherworld.) The following evening the helpless and weak prisoner watches from his window as Count Orlock departs for Bremen. Realizing the dangers that his wife and friends are facing, the clerk, in a superhuman effort, escapes and hurries overland to the coastal town, paralleling the vampire's menacing sea voyage. Both monster and man arrive at the same time, but Harker is unable to prevent the creature's reign of death. For what must have been reasons of expediency, Galeen indicates that there is only one way to rid the world of the pestilence and disease which the vampire obviously represents. The screenwriter has Nina read a book on vampires which states that only a woman pure of heart who offers her blood willingly to the vampire will be able to keep him distracted long enough for the early morning rays of the sun to strike him dead. Realizing that she must give up her life to save that of her husband's, she sends Jonathan away on an errand and lures Orlock to her room. With the crowing of the cock signalling the vampire's doom, the wife's sacrifice saves the villagers as well as Harker. The film ends with a symbolic shot of Castle Orlock destroyed.

Murnau's direction and Fritz Arno Wagner's photography, although failing to hide the meager production budget, suggested the values of making movies out-of-doors and in the actual settings. This was a unique move since their contemporaries were committed to producing films made entirely on murky studio sets. As the scenes in *Nosferatu* passed from the Baltic coast to the Carpathian countryside, the film makers, through the use of odd camera angles and carefully designed long shots, captured the marvels of the open but sinister terrain, the oppressive evilness of medieval castles, with their terrifying staircases, spacious chambers and high archways, the terror of empty village streets with houses crowded next to each other, and the overwhelming feeling of fear and horror in broad daylight. Equally effective were the special effects that Murnau devised to strengthen the visual image of terror: negative filmstrips to dramatize the haunting ride in the phantom coach that takes Harker to his destiny; the stop-start-stop technique which stylized the unnaturalness of the trip; the mysterious opening and closing of large doors; and most memorable of all, Orlock's eerie voyage on the ghost ship filled with rats and vanishing men.

Many critics, not altogether unjustly, have attacked the clumsy editing, the dated acting techniques, and the nonsensical motivations. Then, too, the few studio shots used were far too crude for this period in film history, particularly when Germany prided herself on technical virtuosity. But those who attack the film overlook the artistry of the ideas and the boldness of the director's skill which would mature within a few years to provide the screen with some of its finest motion pictures.

No discussion of significant terror films made during these rare times in the German cinema would be complete without returning to the former Viennese art student Fritz Lang, who had wandered into films in 1916 as a writer, and had so impressed Pommer that the great impresario soon provided him with suitable directing opportunities.

By 1922, Lang had married Thea von Harbou, one of the most famous of all women scenarists, and the two began working on a series of controversial motion pictures, the first important one being released at the same time that *Nosferatu* appeared. The film, *Doctor Marbuse,* was distributed in two parts—*The Great Gambler* and *Inferno.* This five-hour long model of the terrifying super-criminal who seeks to build his vicious organization into a major force for world domination came complete with fascinating disguises, horrifying murders, and exciting gang fights. Being a fast-action moving picture, it was far more successful commercially than any of the other artistic films so far discussed, principally because the audiences enjoyed not only the technical skill but the presentation as well, or as one film historian so aptly put it, "Splendid entertainment."

The year 1923 saw Delca merge with UFA, Pommer made chief of all production, and Lang sky-rocketing to fame over the next two years. Then in 1925, both he and Pommer came to the United States to study American film production methods, which kept them in Hollywood no longer than eight weeks. But the significance of the trip was over before they ever stepped off the boat. Late one evening as their ship waited clearance from the immunization authorities, Lang for the first time viewed the glittering lights of the New York skyline. Astonished by the brilliant spectacle, he started then and there designing a new film, a parable for the present generation about the face of the future.

With its fantastic sets and massive cast, the production cost of *Metropolis* nearly bankrupted UFA the following year. Von Harbou's script was far below her usual standards. This time the melodramatic action took place in a futuristic city, which rested above an underground community of robotized, dehumanized people whose wretched lives were spent in caring for the merciless machines that operated the glittering Metropolis. As the slave labor force grows impatient, one among them, a beautiful girl named Maria, speaks of the need for love and patience, predicting that a mediator will come to bring labor and management together. She not only convinces them of her faith, but also convinces the son of the controller of the great city; the youth's wild idealism forces him to forsake the comfort of his luxurious life to work in the subterranean world of the machines. Meanwhile, John Frederson, the master of Metropolis, becomes increasingly apprehensive about Maria's influence on the workers, and decides to disrupt the growing threat to his position by commissioning the evil scientist Rotwang to construct a humanoid double of the girl who will then incite the duped laborers into revolting and thus provide Frederson with justification for more oppressive measures. The plan almost works. The false Maria leads the toilers of the deep against the monstrous machines, but their misdirected fury results in the flooding of their own city. Only the fortunate appearance of the real Maria, the industrialist's son, and a loyal friend saves the workers' children. The climax comes when the female robot is burned at the stake, the mad, Caligari-like Rotwang is killed, and the industrialist and laborers are united by the father's recognition of the need for love among all men.

Discounting the embarrassingly naïve plot and poor acting, both spectators and critics alike were deeply impressed by the breathtaking architecture of a futuristic age, of a large palatial upper city filled with flying taxis, monorails and towering skyscrapers; and of a lower city, devoid of sunlight, where masses of workers stylized in the Reinhardt stage tradition, moved lifelessly toward a horror of transformers, generators, massive dials and giant clocks. Just as imaginative were the visual effects when Rotwang captures Maria in a shadow-and-light chase through the underground passages, and creates the female humanoid in a superb laboratory sequence filled with shooting currents, electrical switches and ominous controls; and the spectacular shots of the children being rescued from a watery grave.

Particularly noteworthy as well were the superb visual effects created by Karl Freund's ingenious photography. By using special effects, the result of a superb process of mirrored shots developed by a master German technician Eugen Schufftan, the cameraman expertly blended aspects of the real set with minature art work and scale models into convincing scenes of unforgettable design. So powerful was the overall impact of *Metropolis* that Hitler, later, offered Lang the position of director of the Nazi film industry. Although the great director never trafficked in fascism, his wife, whom he later divorced, consented to help the madman's film aspirations.

In 1928, Lang dispelled any notion about his science-fiction skill when he conceived probably the last great German terror film: *Woman in the Moon*. Although no one today would be impressed by the story of a manned rocket flight to the moon in search of gold, the technical virtuosity of the rocket design and the scientific discussion of the moon itself were realistic enough to warrant certain Nazi officials to try to destroy all existing prints lest the film be studied by allied intelligence.

By this time, the accomplishments of the German cinema were played out and very few of her major artists remained in the country. But the years from 1913 to 1928 had provided the terror film with some of its most basic conventions, fundamental lighting techniques, and special effects photography. And if Dr. Kracauer was right, then once and for all Germany had established evidence of the inescapable link between a perennial terror theme and its popularity at the box office, indicating not that these tales are the whims of individual movie-makers, but that they are the visual projections of our subconscious feelings about the world and man's place in it.

The legendary Golem of Jewish folklore is brought to life in this 1920 version
that starred Paul Wegener as the tormented monster.

The opening and closing sequences of *The Cabinet of Dr. Caligari* take place in an insane asylum. Here is the young and sick Francis telling his story to a fellow inmate. (HERMAN G. WEINBERG COLLECTION)

Dr. Caligari explains his side show to the curious spectators. Note how the sets suggest the twisted world in which the characters exist.

(HERMAN G. WEINBERG COLLECTION)

Here, in a scene from *The Cabinet of Dr. Caligari*, Cesare (Conrad Veidt) has to leave the unconscious heroine (Lil Dagover) if he is to escape the pursuing crowd. (THE BETTMANN ARCHIVE, INC.)

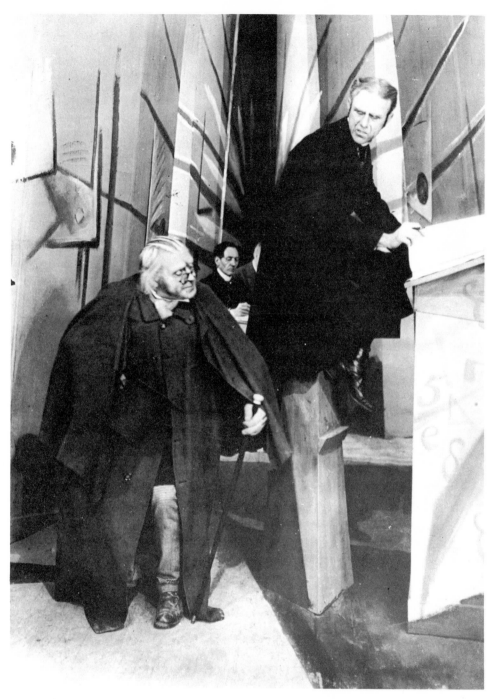

In this scene, the bespectacled Dr. Caligari (Werner Krauss) is insulted by the arrogant town clerk. The painted flat canvases in the background suggest the distorted picture of society that the film-makers wanted to present. Another example of this expressionistic method was the exaggerated desk and chair of the town clerk. (THE BETTMANN ARCHIVE, INC.)

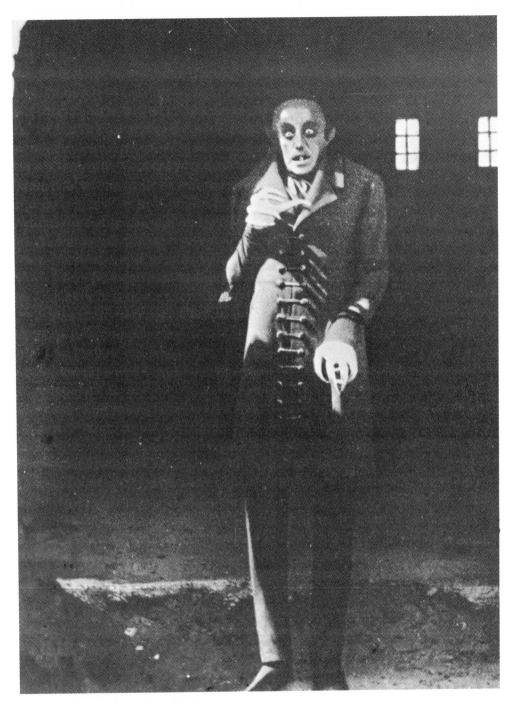

Max Schreck as Count Orlock in *Nosferatu* (1922) welcomes his unsuspecting house guest.   (HERMAN G. WEINBERG COLLECTION)

Max Schreck's performance and make-up for his role as Count Orlock in *Nosferatu* are considered by many film historians to be one of the most sinister terror images ever created. (THE BETTMANN ARCHIVE, INC.)

The dehumanized workers in *Metropolis* (1926).   (HERMAN G. WEINBERG COLLECTION).

A THOUSAND FACES

Methods of projecting horror on the screen rarely differ from country to country, let alone from generation to generation, primarily because there are no geographical or historical patents on terror or talent. And while the German movie industry produced many important terror films dealing with supernatural beings, somber, sinister sets, and violent deaths, she was not alone in her fascination with the macabre. Such countries as Sweden, Denmark, and France also dabbled in the legends and fantasies of spine-tingling melodramas. But more often than not, these motion pictures, like those of Germany's fabled cinema, were artistically interesting but financially embarrassing. The major concern among motion picture people everywhere was how to combine the graphic potential of the monster with the commercial profit at the box office. No one was more involved with those problems than the United States film industry.

Hardly eight years had passed since Henderson's version of *Dr. Jekyll and Mr. Hyde* had been exhibited, but the American cinema had gone through a tremendous revolution.

Edison, Selig and Thanhouser had disappeared from the scene, and yet movies had grown to such prominence that they were now the fifth largest business in the land. Most film companies had migrated west to the perennial sunshine and spacious surroundings of Hollywood. Then, too, the methods of production along with the management of film affairs had radically changed.

One reason for the revolutionary changes was the gluttonus aspirations of the movie moguls themselves. These controversial entrepreneurs were cynical, free-wheeling and daring extroverts who were after big money. They thrived on the challenges of competition and conflict; no risk was too great if it meant not only getting to the top of the industry but also staying there. By 1920, hardly more than a dozen men controlled one of the most powerful entertainment media in the history of mankind: the Warner brothers (Harry, Abe, Sam and Jack), Jesse Lasky, Marcus Loew, Samuel Goldwyn, William Fox, Adolph Zukor, Nicholas and Joseph Schenck, Carl Laemmle, Louis B. Mayer, David Bernstein and Richard Rowland. Their basic formula for success was the same: make it bigger, better and quicker at the lowest price possible!

To achieve their ends, these intriguing impresarios had replaced their haphazard factory methods and run-down stone-front nickelodeons of former days with elaborately organized studios and ornately-built movie theaters. Lighting and camera techniques were all updated; carbonarc flood lights were added to the old Copper-Hewitt floodlights, along with sun-arcs, twin-arc broadsides and a wide variety of different sized reflectors, diffusers and spotlights. An impressive range of camera lenses, filters, gauzes and most important of all, emphasis on the moving camera became standard operating features on all studio sets.

Another reason for the dramatic and important changes was the involvement of Wall Street in movie matters. These financiers, besides being interested in substantial profits, considered the cinema a great asset in their war against communism, illiteracy and immorality. So when the ambitious film-makers sought rich investors for their dream products, Big Business stepped in. And before anyone knew what had happened, the motion picture industry suddenly found itself in the grasp of an empire-building war.

On one side were the eastern money men, seeking security in the form of real estate, efficiency and expediency. These conservative elements were able, for example, to remove Samuel Goldwyn from the presidency of his own company, because of his whimsical and extravagant decisions, particularly the one that motivated him to distribute and exhibit the commercially unpopular film, *The Cabinet of Dr. Caligari*. On the other side were the daring and reckless movie men, seeking wealth in the risky but thrilling world of artists, innovators and hunches. The results of the financial wars were varied, the casualties many. Probably the hardest hit were the foreign film industries, who lost almost all of their talented people, each one coming to Hollywood in search of spectacular salaries and quickly made promises of ideal working conditions. If there were to be any advances in the horrors of the screen, they now had to come from the New World.

The first important terror film of the post-war period in America was made in 1920 at Paramount's Long Island, New York, studios, and it maintained the industry's traditional ties to the theater and to *Dr. Jekyll and Mr. Hyde*.

The director was John Stuart Robinson, an intelligent and ardent gentleman whose dignified style reflected his years of training in the refined conventions of the stage. In spite of his limited success since coming to films five years earlier, Robinson's techniques blended nicely with the American cinema's basic emphasis on narrative motion pictures. If foreigners were bent on developing the film's abilities to examine psychological and atmospheric situations, fine! The U.S. preferred a good, smooth, visual story. And Robinson was particularly adept at creating polished and sensible screenplays which were noted for their simple but dramatic touches of mood, decor and characterization. His film adaptation of the Stevenson work not only brought him his first major triumph, but also provided the silent era with its finest screen version of the popular tale.

In addition to the picture's thrilling and effective use of camera angles, lighting and editing, the script had two fundamental changes from its predecessors. In order to make Hyde a more villainous character, his criminal activities were expanded from that of the senseless child-killer found in the original story to that of a sadistic sex fiend who torments women, especially the sensuous entertainer of a disreputable London hangout, whom he eventually murders. This perverse aspect of his personality gave a more modern dimension to Hyde's evilness as well as a striking visual comparison between the two natures of Dr. Jekyll, who in his more rational moments was engaged to a charming and noble lady. Another change was to invest the good doctor with a sinister advisor, Sir George Carewe, who encouraged the innocent young man to satisfy his baser instincts. This new character was based upon the Lord Henry figure of Oscar Wilde's *The Picture of Dorian Gray*, and Robinson borrowed freely a number of incidents and actual lines from the book. In some ways, this method of incorporating several different literary villains into a single film foreshadowed the house of monster movies of future decades.

But the film's tremendous popularity has to be credited mainly to the superb performance by one of the world's foremost stage actors, John Barrymore. In 1920, at the peak of his film career, having already made thirteen movies and now established as an important screen star, he was intensely interested in the absurd dual characterization which demanded ingenious make-up and melodramatic acting. No one in that age surpassed his ability to present visual distinctions between the scientist and the savage. As Jekyll, he was elegant, clean-shaven and very regal. But as Hyde, Barrymore transformed his handsome features into gruesome, disheveled shapes.

Most impressive of all were his conversion scenes where Barrymore played upon his unique theatrical training. Naturally the first transformation was the best. Secluded in his private laboratory, he quietly mixed an ominous formula, poured himself a dose, and sat at his large desk, positioning his full face toward the audience. Slowly he raised the bubbling contents to his lips, paused slightly, and then swallowed the chemicals in a single gulp. A few seconds elapsed. The camera remained fixed on the actor, whose face began to contort and whose body began to stiffen. Having suggested that the formula was taking effect, Barrymore fell from his chair out of sight, leaving one hand on the desk, clearly in view. At this point, the great actor had help from his cameraman, who made a three-foot fade out, waited while the actor's hand was carefully outlined on the desktop, and then backed up the exposed film three feet. All was in readiness when Barrymore, now made-up as the demented Hyde, repositioned himself behind the desk, at the same time placing his fang-like hand in the marked position. The transformation effect was made in the camera itself by signalling the actor to emerge on the cameraman's cue, a strenuous and discomforting feat which forced Barrymore to one-handedly push himself up from the floor. Nevertheless, audiences were thrilled with the dissolve from the dignified face to the grotesque image that appeared before their eyes, and Barrymore, egocentric star that he was, allowed the viewers to stare for a few more moments at his bizarre disguise. Then the director cut to a long shot of the gruesome being grabbing his cane and heading out for a night of terror.

So successful was this particular version that a few weeks after it was released, Louis B. Mayer tried to put out a quickly made imitation to cash in on Barrymore's triumph but the cheapness of the production plus the happy ending of Jekyll awaking from a dream quickly discouraged any one from seeing it. After that no one tried to film the tale again during the silent era.

In spite of the audience's obvious fascination with such stories, Paramount failed to realize that it had in its studios a free-lance performer destined to become the first great terror star of motion pictures. Lon Chaney, "the man of a thousand faces," was then a minor actor-writer-director who had just received some rave notices for his stunning pantomimes in *The Miracle Man* (1919), as Frog, the pseudo-cripple, whose lifeless limbs are "miraculously" healed.

Chaney's mastery of pantomime owed much to the knowledge and emotional maturity he had gained as the son of a deaf-mute parents. Out of necessity and desire, the young boy became adept at communicating with them through sign language, charades and facial expressions. His unbelievable skill with the art of make-up also developed out of desire and necessity. In those primitive days of films, steady work was very hard to come by for relatively unknown personalities, and Chaney regularly checked the casting lists for unusual parts. Because he wanted to act as often as possible, he equipped himself with a portable make-up kit, and experimented with different disguises, all designed to fit the films being shot at the time. Between 1913 and 1919, the ingenious artist appeared in well over a hundred parts. When he couldn't find employment that way, he managed to earn some extra money by directing a film or writing a scenario. Very few stars ever worked as hard for their fame as did Mr. Chaney.

His first break in terror films came in 1922, with director Wallace Worsley's *A Blind Bargain,* another example of the movie industry's obsession with mad scientists. This time the action involved a misguided investigator's experiments with animal tissues, resulting in mutated ape-men, clinical disasters, and a body-crushing climax. Chaney's dual role as the evil scholar and his pathetic hunchbacked assistant added considerably to the growing list of mad scientist conventions.

Then in 1923, again with Worsley directing, Chaney reached stardom as the pitiful, repulsive bellringer of Notre Dame. The film was based upon Victor Hugo's classic romance of medieval days, where a number of lives all centered on a deformed and miserable hunchback who haunted the vast halls of the great church. The main players were Esmeralda, the enchanting gypsy dancer who loved the gallant Captain Phoebus de Chateaupers, the lecherous Archdeacon's brother Jehan whose uncontrollable passion almost destroys the two lovers, and Quasimodo, a creature of the cathedral whom the Parisians of that day called "The Hunchback of Notre Dame." His devotion to Esmeralda eventually saves her life at the expense of his own.

Here was the art of the silent screen as it had rarely been seen before: spectacular and massive sets, outstanding lighting, intriguing camera work, excellent mob scenes, a strong script and breathtaking sequences. With it all, Chaney still emerged as the most memorable sight.

Opening with some impressive long shots of the magnificently constructed Notre Dame, various shots were then shown of the giant church square where the oppressed citizens of Paris met once each year to enjoy themselves. Each of the important characters was singled out, introducing his strengths and weaknesses. And then there was a close-up shot of the hunchback, high up on the cathedral wall, hands tucked under his chin, pensive, deaf, half-blind—isolated from everything except his beloved ringing church bells. From then on, Chaney dominated the action, swinging from gargoyles, sliding down beautiful pillars, ringing the giant bells, being crowned king of the fools, getting whipped in public, and pouring molten lead down on an angry mob.

His make-up was superb. Chaney wore shoulder pads (like those of football players) and attached to them a breastplate for his chest and a 70-pound hump for his back. Over these he placed a light leather harness, which when hooked up, forced Chaney to walk hunched over. To cover the harness, he donned a tinted rubber suit, covered with long, animal hair. He also used special mortician's putty to disfigure his face, a popping false eye, a set of fanglike teeth together with some undisclosed material so that he couldn't close his mouth, and a grotesque wig, matted with bristly hair. And for close to eighty-nine days, Lon Chaney, in excruciating pain, hobbled around the Universal set.

Fortunately for everyone connected with the movie, Carl Laemmle had placed a brilliant young man of twenty-two— Irving Thalberg—in charge of Universal's west coast studios. The extraordinary executive saw in the finished print of *The Hunchback of Notre Dame* a great movie and refused to go along with the original distributing contracts. He reckoned on Laemmle's overriding concern that production costs determine how a film gets exhibited. Thalberg, in a daring gamble, made Worsley reassemble the cast for some further crowd shots, thereby escalating the film's financial outlay by approximately $150,000. The idea paid off. When the president saw the final sum, he initiated a tremendous advertising program to ballyhoo the picture's merits. So it was that Lon Chaney finally became a full-fledged star.

The next and last important terror film that Chaney made for Universal was a screen adaptation of Gaston Leroux's 1908 mystery romance, *The Phantom of the Opera*.

The motion picture was completed under very trying circumstances, mainly because of director Rupert Julian's temperamental flareups. After a number of heated arguments, innumerable script changes which required unexpected shootings, character additions and omissions, Laemmle replaced Julian with Edward Sedgwick, and the third version of the yet undistributed film was exhibited for the first time in 1925.

The narrative followed very closely the plot of the novel: A scarred and bitter musician, Eric Claudin, secretly dwells in the lower depths of the opera house, harassing and killing those who oppose his whims while he seeks to win the love of the beautiful, young and talented Christine. In spite of the flawed finished print, there are many exquisite moments in the movie, which begins backstage of the ornate building where the graceful ballet dancers and the humorous stagehands exchange rumors about a mysterious ghost—a phantom —that haunts the building, blackmails the owners with threats of sudden disasters, and occupies the reserved "Box 5" at all performances. The suspense builds as we catch a fleeting glimpse of the back of a ghostlike figure in evening clothes watching an opera. Next we see his shadow on the wall as his melodious voice secretly instructs the unsuspecting singer, Christine, in her art. Then we see his gloved hand as it tosses a threatening note onto the owners' desk, warning them not to allow the present star to continue in the company and demanding that Christine take her place. The star, Carlotta, refuses to be intimidated, but that evening as she performs in *Faust*, the house lights flicker, and then, in what many film historians consider one of the finest moments in all of the silent cinema, the great crystal chandelier comes crashing down on the audience, and the people flee in panic down the long, wide opera steps. The phantom, still unseen by us, lures Christine to him. In one brilliant shot, the suddenly timid hand of the terrorist hesitates in touching the innocent soprano's shoulder. Then it's done and she turns to see that her mentor and the phantom are one. But he is masked, and we still are allowed to imagine what lies behind the covering.

Eric takes the frightened Christine with him down through brilliant examples of filmic composition: the multiple arched levels of the catacombs, across the underground canal to a mysteriously opened door, and into an exquisitely furnished chamber, where the now all-too-human creature pleads on bended knees for her love and understanding. The bewildered and trapped girl has no choice but to remain with him, although her feelings of repulsion begin to turn to those of sympathy for such a forlorn human being. Later, while Eric is seated at his grand organ, playing his original composition, "Don Juan Triumphant," she foolishly steals to his side to discover his hidden identity and rips off his disguise, and we are finally allowed to see the face of horror. Now desperate, Christine pleads for her freedom, which the compassionate phantom grants on the condition that she remain faithful to him and not reveal his identity.

A few days later at the annual masked ball, she breaks her promise, and on the opera roof the terrified ingenue confides in her true love. But Eric, disguised as the spectral Red Death, hovers over them, perched on an enormous baroque statute, listening to every unguarded word. The next evening, he kidnaps Christine, and what follows are some of the most bizarre devices ever jam-packed into so short a quickly approaching conclusion: sliding panels, trap doors, torture chambers, underwater tubes for murderers to breathe by, rooms filled with gunpowder to blow up the opera house, torchlight chases, attempted escapes by carriage (past the old Notre Dame set, which was still standing).

Chaney, truly remarkable, was aided considerably by the novelty of Technicolor. For many years, even before Méliès, artists tried tinting and toning methods to highlight special effects. By 1923, color experiments had progressed to the stage where technicians using a specially designed split-beam system were able to produce striking red and green images on celluloid. This two-color break-through, later to be improved in the thirties, was used to considerable advantage in the ballet, *Faust,* and masked ball sequences.

Once again, however, Chaney's brilliant make-up provided the most enduring effects. Although he was reluctant to discuss exactly how the face of horror was actually constructed, historians seem to agree that his nostrils were expanded with pins, his face painted an eerie white with dark black marks under his eyes, clamps to hold back his lips and fitted false teeth, while special disks were inserted in his mouth to disfigure his cheekbones. Furthermore, his skull was elongated with a matted wig at the top. Many critics of the era claimed that the full figure of the Phantom was the most terrifying in all silent film.

What made Chaney greater than any of the other performers who provided horror on the screen was his gift for communicating pity for even the most repulsive of human creatures, for evoking some sympathetic response for the pathetic outcasts whose most villainous actions stemmed from their passionate need for love and kindness. As one perceptive critic has pointed out, it seemed as if Chaney, sensing the disillusionment of his generation with the ways of mankind, sought to remind us that only through understanding, sympathy and genuine affection could we hope to survive.

In 1925, the finest science-fiction terror film of the era before movies began to speak was released—*The Lost World.* Based upon a tale by Sir Arthur Conan Doyle, the film concerned a scientific expedition led by none other than Professor Challenger, and included in his party were the by-now-familiar members of the popular love triangle—the beautiful girl, the adventurous aristocrat and the dashing journalist. The action begins slowly as the group arrives at a foreboding uncharted island—suddenly they come face to face with prehistoric beasts. Then mayhem breaks out: unbelievable battles between gigantic creatures of the Stone Age, death-defying exploits by brave men, and a grand capture of a monstrous brontosaurus. The proud explorers return to London with their prize, hoping for fame and fortune. Instead, the savage denizen frees himself and nearly destroys the city before his slips away to his "virgin world," as the advertising campaign described it.

What made the movie one of the ten best of the year was the brilliant technical skill of Willis O'Brien and the superb photography of Arthur Edeson. Together, they so perfected O'Brien's research in slow motion photography and miniature rubber figures, that the two men were able to integrate scaled sets, movable models, live actors and special laboratory processes successfully into a breathtaking world of terror. We will come back to O'Brien in the next chapter, because as many of you may have guessed, the plots, incidents, and techniques were expanded eight years later, into the grandest science-fiction movie of all time: *King Kong*.

By the end of 1925, Thalberg and Chaney were at M-G-M, and the great star had begun work with another Universal import, Tod Browning. The results were evident in a number of films containing terror effects. The reason may well have been that as a director Browning cared little for sensible stories or well-developed characterizations. For him, movies offered a unique opportunity to dramatize the absurd and to experiment with special effects. Their best film together came in 1927, *London After Midnight*, where Chaney again played a dual role: a fake vampire and a Scotland Yard inspector.

In that same year, which also ended the silent days of film, the final significant terror film of that era was made by a German director—Paul Leni—then working at Universal studios, who used a scenario based upon a London play, *The Bat*.

The setting of the movie, *The Cat and the Canary*, took place at midnight in a strange, isolated mansion kept by a sinister housekeeper who welcomed a number of greedy relatives to the reading of a will twenty years after the writer's death. Before dawn, the lawyer had been murdered, strange hands crept out of hidden panels, mysterious passageways were discovered, curtains billowed in every room, a mad doctor invaded the house, and the least likely relative had turned out to be the unknown killer. Most of the incidents, sets and camera work eventually became standard features of all the haunted houses of movies yet to come. Much of the credit goes to the director, who skillfully filled the picture with appropriate thrilling moments.

For over thirty years, artists had worked on the macabre silent picture and now it was over. Behind them they had left a host of impressive films. To some of us the techniques may now seem crude, the acting somewhat dated and the effects rather unconvincing. But for many others, the terror is as real today as it was then.

Lon Chaney's Make-up

You have often wondered how the famous character actor could portray such terrifically ugly Chinamen. These pictures tell you. Directly below, he is putting on one of his wigs. The wig is the simplest part of it.

The oriental slant to the eyes is obtained by tape drawn tightly away from the optics. Mr. Chaney is performing this painstaking operation above. You may also glance over his make-up table, which boasts every conceivable kind of wig, eye-brow and eye-lash outfit and teeth.

YOU have seen him as a Chinaman, an Indian — eastern and western; a Russian Grand Duke, a Bowery crook, a half-breed, and a madman. Sometimes you don't even recognize him, and wonder where the director got such a realistic type. Lon Chaney has won distinction and the title of master of make-up and a substantial salary and finally stardom through his ability to impersonate every character under the cooper-hewitts.

The hideous effects achieved by Chaney are mostly due to the teeth he wears. These are real teeth which he places over his own and which make him the ugliest man in the movies! (Of course, Lon Chaney is really an awfully nice chap and exceedingly popular in the Hollywood film colony. But he says if this is generally known it will ruin his screen reputation.)

The greatest screen terrorist of the silent era. Reprinted from *Photoplay* magazine, March 1922. (THE BETTMANN ARCHIVE, INC.)

In *The Hunchback of Notre Dame* (1923), Lon Chaney gave an excellent performance as the frightening but pitiful Quasimodo. Nigel de Brulier plays the saintly-looking priest.   (THE BETTMANN ARCHIVE, INC.)

(*right*) In the 1957 French version of *The Hunchback of Notre Dame*, Anthony Quinn played the bell-ringer. It hardly compared to the previous classic combinations of spectacle and horror created by Chaney and Laughton.   (BETTMANN/SPRINGER FILM ARCHIVE)

Charles Laughton as the pathetic bell-ringer in the 1939 version of *The Hunchback of Notre Dame.*   (CULVER PICTURES, INC.)

In *The Phantom of the Opera* (1925) Lon Chaney, as the mutilated Eric Claudin, suffered incredible pain to create this terrifying image. He inserted hooks in his nostrils and stretched his nose by tieing hooks to his wig. This helped create a skeleton effect.　(THE BETTMANN ARCHIVE, INC.)

(*right*) A terrifying moment in screen history occurred when Christine (Mary Philbin) unmasked the phantom of the opera (Lon Chaney). He is now explaining to her that there is no hope of rescue.

(BETTMANN/SPRINGER FILM ARCHIVE)

Disguised as the Red Death, Eric (Lon Chaney) attends the masked ball in *The Phantom of the Opera*.   (THE BETTMANN ARCHIVE, INC.).

The comic-horror movie *The Cat and the Canary* (1927) became the model for a popular plot in terror films, that of the madman who tries to drive his victims insane. In this scene, comedian Creighton Hale has just fainted at the sight of villain Forrest Stanley in his cat-like disguise.

(THE BETTMANN ARCHIVE, INC.)

Claude Rains hid his acid-scarred face behind this mask in the 1943 version of *The Phantom of the Opera*. Although the movie won an Academy Award for its lush Technicolor photography, many of the chilling horror effects of the Chaney original were missing. (BETTMANN/SPRINGER FILM ARCHIVE)

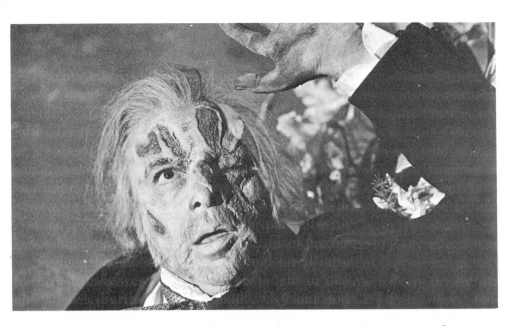

In this 1962 version of *The Phantom of the Opera,* Herbert Lom tried unsuccessfully to recapture the element of terror that had so long been associated with the tragic tale of Eric Claudin.

Lon Chaney as the disguised vampire in *London After Midnight* (1927).

A TIME OF KINGS

The coming of the "talkies" once more turned the movie world upside down, and with that great technical revolution, the art of the terror film improved beyond anyone's wildest expectations. Before 1927, the silent films had frightened us with their skillful editing and brilliant visual compositions. But now the sound movies created a magnificent new dimension, one that could capitalize on synchronized music, actual speech, clever sound effects, highly trained speaking voices, and an intriguing use of silence. The future looked extremely promising.

Naturally, the initial attempts at producing sound pictures were primitive. These movies were filled with oversimplified plots, ridiculous motivations, flat characterizations, poorly synchronized sounds, trite dialogue and static action. Yet each failure was a significant step forward, a trial-and-error method of film-making which offered an excellent opportunity for the old masters to adjust to the new possibilities as well as an exciting chance for a young corps of artists to develop their special talents. Within a decade, innovative and creative men would produce some of the most marvelous terror films the world had yet seen.

The first major horror breakthrough came from the efforts of Tod Browning, whose lifelong association with fantasy and the supernatural earned him his reputation as "the Edgar Allan Poe of the movies." Even though he had demonstrated a number of times during the twenties his remarkable artistic abilities with film, Browning rarely knew what he would do next. For the most part his unique talents were unappreciated and his growing addiction to alcohol marked him as an undesirable employee to Hollywood's conservative studio heads. Then in 1930, thanks to the perceptive Thalberg and the talented Chaney, Browning made a successful sound version of his popular silent film *The Unholy Three.* As a result of the picture's obvious box-office appeal, Universal Studios contracted him to make a talking version of Stoker's *Dracula,* to star Lon Chaney. Browning was delighted. Unfortunately the magnificent master of repulsive make-up died of cancer before production could begin.

Plans for the picture, however, had progressed too far to cancel the project. A suitable replacement for the vampire role had to be found. Luckily, Browning knew someone, a character actor who had played a minor part in one of his films the previous year, a Hungarian artist who had performed the Dracula role in a 1927 stage version of the Gothic tale. So it was that the forty-eight-year-old Arisztid Olt— better known as Bela Lugosi—came to the screen role that was to be his namesake for over three decades.

Lugosi was an unusual man, an uneven performer and the first true screen aristocrat of terror films. A comparison with his predecessor is inevitable. To Chaney, the audience gave sympathy and understanding. Lugosi, on the other hand, by his mannerisms and appearance, demanded rather than earned fear. Vanity more than anything else encouraged him to avoid facial make-up as much as possible, preferring to adorn himself in evening clothes and terrorize in elegance. And while Chaney dwelled on the tragic horrors that life could bring to the grotesque, Lugosi enthralled you with the sinister charm of the living dead.

Universal, continuing its long interest in the macabre and always ready for a delightful bit of irony, premiered *Dracula* on Saint Valentine's Day in 1931 at the sumptuous Roxy Theater, where one and all came to see the exciting adventures of the blood-sucking ghoul of the Carpathian countryside. To today's viewers, much of the film's famed ability to frighten and terrify people seems grossly exaggerated. Many of the scenes are poorly designed, the acting rather stilted, and the action, slow-moving and simplified. These are the period's and the film's indefensible artistic flaws.

To dismiss *Dracula* as a failure by present-day standards, however, is a serious viewing error. The movie has many valuable and rewarding moments. Karl Freund's work, for example, deserves particular consideration. The great German cameraman, who had collaborated so brilliantly with Murnau and Lang, created some marvelous atmospheric scenes of Count Dracula's foreboding castle, with its sticky cobwebs, sinister catacombs, and unholy occupants. Then too, there are many outstanding moving camera shots and carefully composed camera angles that add considerably to the subjective state of the victims' fearful encounters.

Equally rewarding is the visual study of Professor Stoker's fascinating account of vampirism, brought very carefully to fruition in the book, the play and now on the screen. In particular, Browning emphasized the characterization of the elderly and shrewd Professor Van Helsing, whose lifelong research and unflinching courage proved to be Dracula's undoing.

Also valuable is a close look at the film script, which established for decades to come the screen traditions of the living dead. Here we see a Count Dracula, having lived for centuries off the blood of the now depopulated and weak Balkan citizenry, forced to leave his Carpathian stronghold, in a perilous search for new and richer resources. The arrival of an unfortunate real estate agent provides the vampire with the idea of draining London. Soon the Count, having secretly settled both his coffin and himself in a suitable cellar, begins dining on a number of unsuspecting young women. Fortunately for the British, Professor Van Helsing is able to convince the right people that he knows a considerable amount about the supernatural powers of vampires, their unusual sleeping habits, and the means by which the loathsome creatures can be destroyed. With the aid of crosses, stakes, and sunlight, Van Helsing makes his point. In this oversimplified version of *Dracula* are several of the basic patterns to be found in many of the later vampire stories: helpless heroines robed in their white nightgowns (almost as if they were brides of horror), suspenseful moments as the sinister ghouls descend on their victims (most of whom try a number of recommended vampire preventatives such as crosses, charms and special herbs), and the basic protagonist-antagonist relationship between the scholar and the evil being (with the academician always winning).

Browning made just two more significant films over the next twenty-nine years, both for Metro-Goldwyn-Mayer. In 1933, he directed the strange story of the beautiful trapeze artist Cleopatra, whose macabre treatment of the dwarf Hans brings on the incredible vengeance of the circus mutations. *Freaks*, although dealing with several grotesque and very sensitive situations, is one of the few films in the history of the cinema that presents the lives of deformed individuals with sympathy and understanding. *The Mark of the Vampire* (1935) provided a luscious female ghoul to match Lugosi's appetite, and also marked the end of the director's innovating and interesting macabre movies. In 1939, Browning retired from the hectic world of horror films and spent the next twenty-three years of his life enjoying the financial rewards of a screen terrorist.

As for Bela Lugosi, throughout the remainder of his life he too experienced a downward trend, rarely ever again reaching the fame he had achieved as Dracula. Ignored for most of his career by the film companies, continually involved in unhappy marriages, perennially facing financial disasters, the lonely and misunderstood man eventually turned to narcotics. Then, in August of 1956, Lugosi died, like the star he once replaced, of cancer.

By now, Universal Pictures was so delighted in the progress of *Dracula* that even before the film's distribution had gone very far, the studio's story department was looking for another supernatural monster to put into production. One in particular caught the eye of the researchers, a remarkable Gothic novel written in 1816 by a twenty-one-year-old girl: Mary Wollstonecraft Shelley's *Frankenstein*.

Although made in Hollywood, the film classic has a European appearance to it. French director Robert Florey prepared the scenario that relied just as much on the German films *The Golem* and *Homunculus* as it did on the original Shelley romance. Florey's simplified plot, cinematically conceived, told of a scientist's dream of creating human life, and of the terrifying but pathetic monster whose bewildered search for sympathy and love turns him into a creature of evil who is at odds both with the intolerant world around him and with his own suffering self-image. One of the screenwriter's most ingenious touches was to have Baron Frankenstein's deformed assistant (the very talented but unfairly maligned Dwight Frye) accidentally steal a criminal's brain for the secret experiments.

Florey, thinking that he was going to direct the movie, and not just prepare the script, tested Lugosi for the part, but the actor was appalled at the film rushes, which clearly stressed the importance of make-up. The Hungarian turned down the part, reportedly exclaiming that anyone could take the role since the audience never really saw the actual features of the actor.

At this point, James Whale, an English director relatively new to films and Hollywood, saw Lugosi's test shots and asked to see the script, thinking this might contain some interesting material for him to experiment with. Suddenly Florey was off the assignment and Whale was directing *Frankenstein.*

Whale was one of the most brilliant theatrical-men-turned-movie-directors in the history of terror films. Extremely gifted when it came to dramatic staging, wry humor and visual arrangements, the British artist also had a unique talent for casting his moving pictures. He chose Colin Clive, an accomplished English actor with whom he had just finished a film (the director's second up to that time), to play the role of Henry Frankenstein. (No reason was ever given why the experimenter's name was changed from Victor—as it appeared in the book—to Henry.) Whale explained his ideas about the interesting part to Clive in a letter, "I see Frankenstein as an intensely sane person, at times rather fanatical and in one or two scenes a little hysterical . . ." Whale went on to write, "Frankenstein's nerves are all to pieces. He is a very strong, extremely dominant personality, sometimes very soft, sympathetic and decidedly romantic. He hates causing anxiety to Elizabeth and his father, but his passionate zeal and his invention forced him to do so. He is pulled two ways, his love for Elizabeth and his almost insane passion for his experiments . . . There are none of Dracula's manical cackles. I want the picture to be a very modern, materialistic treatment of this medieval story, something of Doctor Caligari and something of Edgar Allan Poe, and, of course, a good deal of us."

The crucial part, obviously, was that of Adam, the monster (nameless in the film). And Whale wanted someone in the role who was similar to Lon Chaney, an actor capable of blending both terror and suffering humanity in a single performance. Legend has it that one eventful day while the director was having lunch in the studio commissary he met a friend of his, William Henry Pratt, a minor middle-aged British actor who worked under the stage name of Boris Karloff. When Whale asked him if he would consider the monster role, Karloff supposedly replied, "A monster indeed!" But he needed work and was not about to turn down a job that promised him $125.00 a week for the next few months. (Universal reportedly made well over fourteen million dollars on Karloff's performance.)

For more than four weeks, Karloff and the genius of Universal's make-up department, Jack Pierce, worked on the monster's appearance. Slowly but surely Mrs. Shelley's emaciated yellowish fiend became a large, clumsy monster, with many human characteristics, but all so distorted in proportion as to make the invention hideous and weird. Heavy-leaden shoes exaggerated his every step; wrist and throat, lined with ugly stitches, emphasized his unnatural origin; ominous electrodes sticking out from both sides of his neck indicated where life was plugged in; and the raised forehead, the matted head, and the freakish face provided the final touches to the most famous of all make-up creations in the history of motion pictures.

In many respects *Frankenstein* was a breath-taking motion picture, although it too suffered from the same artistic problems evident in *Dracula*. Starting from the opening atmospheric shots in a tiny, isolated village graveyard, Whale established a remarkable mood, and increased the effects by carrying the action over to the medieval castle and eventually reaching some of the finest moments in all the terror films in the misguided scientist's secret laboratory. Whale, in excellently designed shots, aided considerably by the distinguished camera work of the experienced Arthur Edeson and the remarkable sets of art designer Herman Rosse, created a marvelous sequence in which Professor Waldman comes to watch his former student's supernatural experiment. At first the cautious scholar and the expelled Frankenstein review the controversial nature of the tests being carried on with ultraviolet rays, dead animals and human transplants. Henry claims that he has gone further than any mortal has yet dared venture, and triumphantly reveals his masterpiece. Dr. Waldman is horrified, and even more skeptical that such a thing can be given life. Then Frankenstein demonstrates how the synthetic man can be created. In a series of thrilling camera angles, extremely well-paced and owing much to the laboratory scenes in *Metropolis,* the unorthodox experimenter mechanically raises the body of the monster to a predetermined opening in the ceiling where flying kites attract the lighting bolts from the raging storm. There in the electrifying darkness of night, sparks, currents, dials, electrodes, and levers capture our eyes. Finally, the nameless creature is lowered back down to the surgical table. Everyone's attention is riveted to the hideous, still bandaged form. The ugly hand of the monster begins to move, and Frankenstein, delirious with joy, screams, "He's alive! He's alive I tell you! He's alive!"

Next we see how the pathetic and disoriented monster suffers from the torments of the scientist's dreadful hunchback servant, how Frankenstein begins to regret his invention, and how the artificial human breaks free and revenges himself on the cruel world about him. Whale highlights the paradox of the monster's internal and external state in the tender encounter with a young child, who is serenely sitting by a lake tossing in flowers which float gently away. For a few moments, the two innocent beings play peacefully together. Soon the ignorant giant accidentally kills his companion by tossing her into the water, thinking there was no difference between the girl and the flowers.

Whale considered a number of conclusions for his macabre movie, finally deciding to destroy the unfortunate monster in a spectacular mill fire, while at the same time allowing the misguided scientist a miraculous escape from death. The motion picture was an instant success, and Karloff, who never received star billing or even an invitation to attend the film's premiere, sky-rocketed to fame as "the unknown actor who had played the monster."

One interesting side-light of the world's sensational impact concerns the narrow tastes of the theater owners of those early days. These silly men arbitrarily decided to delete the shots of the monster throwing the young girl to her death. They considered it too horrifying for "their audiences." Consequently, many versions of *Frankenstein* exhibited today are based upon those censored prints of 1931, and the effects of the taste of a previous age still haunt us now.

Before Universal Studios could make a sequel to its new popular success, Whale and Karloff became involved in a number of new terror projects. The ingenious director in 1932 turned his attention to a fascinating horror story entitled *The Old Dark House,* a remarkable sound picture of the haunted house school of film terror. Based upon J.B. Priestley's book, the movie script centered on a group of strangers who regrettably seek shelter one dark, stormy night in a lonely, foreboding mansion. Once more Whale's outstanding casting talent made the difference between a superficial film and a movie of merit. Some of the performers were Boris Karloff, Melvyn Douglas, Charles Laughton, Ernest Thesiger and Raymond Massey. This may well be the most star-studded production in terror film history.

Next Whale turned his camera toward H.G. Wells' novel about Dr. John Griffin, whose dangerous experiments with sinister drugs eventually cost him his life. The director offered the part to Karloff, but the by-now-established star refused to remain unseen until the final reel, and thus the role eventually fell to fellow British stage actor Claude Rains, who made a sensational debut via his highly trained voice in the 1933 film classic *The Invisible Man.*

Karloff, in the meanwhile, had just completed creating Universal's third major film monster in the 1932 screen terror masterpiece *The Mummy*. This splendid terror motion picture was Karl Freund's first directing venture, and for his basic material he wisely chose the eerie legend of an Egyptian layman, Im-ho-tep, whose disastrous desire for the Princess Ananka destroys his chance for eternal rest. When the beautiful princess dies unexpectedly, the distraught commoner, in defiance of the sacred laws of Amon-Ra, tried to steal the miraculous tara leaves and thereby restore his sweetheart to life everlasting. But the heretic is captured and sentenced by the angry Pharaoh to be buried alive in the Princess' tomb. Even more horrifying, the infidel is denied his last rites. And so it is that Im-ho-tep, clothed in the bandages of the accursed mummy, spends eternity guarding his beloved's corpse.

Freund's stimulating camera work and exquisite visual details added considerably to Karloff's exciting dual role as the ancient mummy and the strange Egyptian Ardath Bey. The conventions of almost all future mummy movies followed the various situations in this film, a plot that relied upon connecting one coincidence with another until the horrible truth became evident to even the dullest of mortals: e.g., the strange encounters between the scholar and the suspicious Egyptian who broods over the glass enclosure of Princess Ananka, the remarkable resemblance between a young heroine and the long-dead princess, the terrifying deaths of people who have seen the living dead, and the eventual recognition scene where the protagonists realize the relationship of Ardath Bey to the 3700-year-old mummy now restored to life. These particular features have stayed with the Egyptian monster films to this very day.

Eventually, the public demanded a return of the Frankenstein monster. Even though they enjoyed the haunted houses, the invisible men, the freaks and the ghouls, one monster above all seemed to satisfy them most. And so in 1935, Universal united Karloff and Whale for the last time in a brilliant sequel, *The Bride of Frankenstein,* probably the most superb production of the story ever made.

The film masterpiece begins with a prologue in which Mary Shelley confides to her audience the startling fact that the monster had not died in the fire, escaping death by submerging himself in the waters surrounding the mill. Fade in to the closing sequences of the original Frankenstein and cut to the murdered girl's father, who, now deranged and vengeful, enters the smouldering ruins to gloat over the charred body of the synthetic man. Suddenly he comes face to face with the unforgettable Karloff, now a more menacing monster because of the additional scars inflicted upon him by the blaze. The enraged creature quickly disposes of his antagonist, then staggers away from the rubble in search of peace.

Soon after, Henry Frankenstein, not satisfied with his narrow escape, agrees to continue his dangerous research with Dr. Pretorious, the scientist who first taught the young student the basic principles of creating life in the laboratory. Now the two men begin anew, this time to create a mate for the monster.

While they are collecting human material for their experiment, the harrassed and frightened creature finds momentary comfort with a blind hermit high up in the mountains. For ever so brief a time, the lonely monster experiences human kindness and understanding. But his idyllic life is interrupted by hunters, and once more he is forced to escape from the world of men. Seeking seclusion in the cemetery late one night, the monster encounters Dr. Pretorious, who comforts the pathetic creature and informs him of the new work being carried on in his behalf. A sinister bond develops between the two.

The chilling climax occurs in a remarkable recreation of the original 1931 laboratory sequence, only this time the monster is present to watch the birth of his bride. In a number of dramatically composed shots, the director reveals how the corpse of a nineteen-year-old girl is brought back to life, only now her beauty is scarred by the crude surgical work of the hysterical scientists. The fiancée, portrayed by Elsa Lanchester, gets one glimpse of her bridegroom and doesn't stop shrieking until the end of the movie. Following her first scream, Karloff begins what many critics considered one of the most tender and moving love scenes in the annals of terror films. Patting her hand, trying every which way to express his deep need for love, and demonstrating how truly kind he can be, the sad, grotesque monster tries to win the heart of his terrified mate, but to no avail. Finally, with a single tear in his eye, realizing at last that there can be no hope for him, he decides to destroy himself, the synthetic woman and Dr. Pretorious. He waits only long enough for Frankenstein and his wife to leave the laboratory before he blows it up.

Without doubt Karloff's poignant interpretation of the tormented monster and Ernest Thesiger's convincing performance as the sinister scientist elevated the film above any of its predecessors or imitators. Considerable credit must also go to James Whale's excellent coordination of an original musical score, elaborate gothic sets and a fluid, moving camera. *The Bride of Frankenstein* still stands today as a very fine example of what truly gifted people can do within the limitations of a commercial and emerging art form.

For Whale, this was the end of a magnificent interest in the terrors of the screen. Although he continued to make movies for the next six years, his retirement at the relatively young age of forty-five in 1941 caused no apparent concern among the makers of horror films. What was strange, however, were a number of mysteries surrounding the man himself: why he stopped his exceptional work in this particular area, why he never again was able to resume a successful film career, and what were the unexplained events that led to his being found dead in his swimming pool in 1957.

So far in this time of kings we have dwelt on the tremendous importance of the great foreign directors, the talented stage actors and the superb technicians collected by Universal Pictures. As a result, our major attention has been focused on the studio's famous monster films: *Frankenstein, Dracula* and *The Mummy*. But now we need to consider, even if only in passing, the movie industry's many other notable terror contributions. Universal, for example, released Florey's praiseworthy adaptation of a Poe story *Murders in the Rue Morgue* (1932), highlighted by Lugosi's impressive performance as a mad scientist experimenting with ape-women. The same studio also did *The Black Cat* (1934), in which the competent Austrian director Edgar Ullmer brought together for the first time the two reigning masters of terror—Karloff and Lugosi—in an intriguing screen melodrama of magic, torture and murder.

Then, too, other major American studios had their special representatives at the court of terror. Metro-Goldwyn-Mayer deserves recognition for its three prize works. Besides Browning's films—*Freaks* and *The Mark of the Vampire*—there was Charles Brabin's *The Mask of Fu Manchu* (1932), featuring the versatile Boris Karloff as the diabolical oriental whose horrendous criminal activities threaten mankind. In addition, Paramount Pictures had two terror classics. One was Rouben Mamoulian's distinguished 1932 version of *Dr. Jekyll and Mr. Hyde,* which boasted that its star Frederic March was the only actor ever to win an Academy Award for a monster film. Then there was Erle Kenton's novel and fantastic *The Island of Lost Souls* (1932). Based upon an H.G. Wells story, the movie had Charles Laughton, the distinguished English stage star, playing the part of a demented scientist who enjoyed transforming beasts into human beings. Warner Brothers, the company that made the first successful talking picture, was only able to create one important terror film, but it was in revolutionary color: Michael Curtiz's *The Mystery of the Wax Museum* (1932). This movie starred another famous British stage actor, Lionel Atwill, as the insane artist whose magnificent wax figures cleverly disguised the corpses of the people he had killed.

Overseas, particularly in Paris, film artists congregated to continue their interest in the macabre and the supernatural. Pommer and Lang, in their self-imposed exile from Germany and just before they left France for the United States, joined with the marvelous Hungarian actor Peter Lorre to create the brilliant movie *M* (1932). This was Lorre's screen debut and his exceptional acting as the child-killer who is finally captured because even the criminal world wants him out of the way typecast the marvelous actor for the rest of his life.

It was in Paris also that the magnificent Danish director Carl T. Dreyer completed what many film historians consider to be the most artistic horror movie of all time: *Vampyr* or *The Strange Adventures of David Gray* (1931). Instead of the well-known Stoker story, Dreyer fashioned his vampire tale on a relatively unknown Irish piece of fiction which told of a female vampire who thrives on the blood of young girls. The screenplay presented a wistful and trance-like world of witches, haunted houses, mysterious messages, and terrifying inhuman relationships.

But of all the terror films made then and now, whether in Europe or America, none has been more widely acclaimed or brought greater satisfaction to critics and viewers alike than RKO's fabulous *King Kong*. Here was the brilliant culmination of all the creative and innovating work in screen illusions up to 1933.

The idea for the movie itself originated in Africa in 1929, during the location shooting for Paramount Pictures' true-life adventure film *Four Feathers*, where Merian C. Cooper

73

and Ernest B. Schoedsack, two expert documentary film-makers, considered combining their mutual interests in adventure films and monster movies. Cooper, in particular, was intrigued with the scheme of making a moving picture about a giant ape he called Kong, based somewhat on a book he had read, *The Dragon Lizards of Komodos*, where giant carnivorous lizards roamed the strange East Indian island.

When Cooper returned to the States, he continued to consider the project and two years later convinced RKO's newly appointed production head, David Selznick, that the film ought to be made. Selznick, in return, suggested that Cooper work with O'Brien, Hollywood's special effects genius, on a test film for the studio's stockholders. The film was shot, emphasizing in one short reel a series of scenes and techniques around which the full-length movie would be based. As a result of that experimental movie, an immediate go-ahead was given in 1931 for *King Kong*, with a budget of over half a million dollars. Cooper contracted Schoedsack to direct the live scenes while he concentrated on the animation sequences with O'Brien. Cooper also contracted the leading lady from *Four Feathers*, Fay Wray, to play the part of the beautiful blonde heroine. He told the actress that she would have as her leading man, ". . . the tallest, darkest man in Hollywood."

O'Brien, in addition to using the many prehistoric models he had created for his silent film *The Lost World*, constructed over twenty different models and shapes of Kong, plus a series of small dolls to represent Fay Wray. Many of his special techniques with the stop-motion action animation remain a secret even today. The guess is that he shot an eighteen inch model, stopped the camera, moved the model about a sixteenth of an inch, and then took another shot. The crew worked at this stop-start pace for almost ten hours every day, feeling quite satisfied if they had completed twenty-five good feet of film for the day's work. Some of the more exciting scenes in the film took considerable time and patience to put on film: Kong's fights with several of the reptiles took about six weeks each, Fay Wray's clinging to a tree trunk in front of a gigantic transparency screen took twenty-two consecutive hours, and the well-known Empire State Building sequence, which used several different processes, required over twenty-three straight shooting hours. Miss Wray herself found much of the work extremely exciting and challenging. In particular, she stressed the close-up problems where she had to be held in Kong's grip, actually a specially constructed ape-hand, eight feet long: "Inside the furry arm there was a steel bar and the whole contraption (with me in hand) could be lowered or raised like a crane. The fingers would be pressed around my waist while I was in a standing position. I would then be raised about ten feet into the air to be lined up with an elevated camera. As I kicked and squirmed and struggled in the ape's hand, his fingers would gradually loosen and begin to open. My fear was real as I grabbed onto his wrist, his thumb, wherever I could, to keep from slipping out of that paw." The lovely star would be rescued for a few moments, then returned to the monster's paw, and the process would be repeated for the remainder of the shooting.

The film's theme was stated right at the beginning with a quotation from an old Arabian proverb, "And the prophet said: 'And lo, the beast looked upon the face of beauty/And it stayed its hand from killing. And from that day, it was as one dead.'" In many respects here was the familiar tale of many previous terror films dealing with the beauty and the beast motif; a frightened, helpless girl rejects the repulsive advances of her monstrous suitor, who, in turn, takes out his frustration on society. Eventually he is killed in a spectacular fall or fire. Shades of *The Golem, Homunculus* and *Frankenstein*! There was another convention that Cooper and Schoedsack employed: empathy for the grotesque monster who is more sinned against than sinning. Many of the tender touches evident in Kong's scenes with the blonde heroine can be traced back to the famous Lon Chaney films like *The Hunchback of Notre Dame* and *The Phantom of the Opera.*

King Kong is not without flaws, and modern viewers often are disappointed in the theatrical staging of the early scenes aboard ship, along with the trite dialogue between the girl and her shipboard lover. Time has a way of changing our tastes. But the scenes of the mighty gorilla engaged in a life and death struggle over and over again rarely fail to satisfy even the most cynical of movie-goers. And as for its hero, one critic said it best when he wrote that Kong is ". . . more than a monster. He is a genuine character, a creature of intelligible rage, nobility of a kind, and above all, pathos. A prehistoric Lear, in a sense . . ."

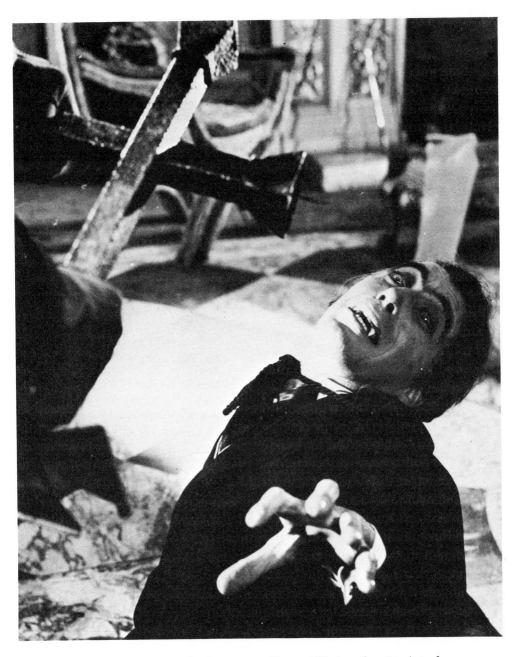

In *The Horror of Dracula*, the sinister Count (Christopher Lee) is shown as he was never seen before, surrounded by more gore, blood and violence than in almost all previous horror movies. (THE BETTMANN ARCHIVE, INC.)

Bela Lugosi in the classic film *Dracula* (1930).

The vampire decides to end the evening festivities in *Vampyr* (1932). Note how Dreyer has used light and shadow to achieve his terror effects.

In this shot from *The Invisible Man,* note the staginess of the 1933 film and the sinister presence of a mysterious stranger (Claude Rains) visible only when covered with bandages and clothes.　(THE BETTMANN ARCHIVE, INC.)

Boris Karloff appears as Ardath Bey, an Egyptian archeologist, in *The Mummy* (1932). Here he is in the Cairo museum, looking down at the corpse of his beloved Princess Ananka.　(BETTMANN/SPRINGER FILM ARCHIVE)

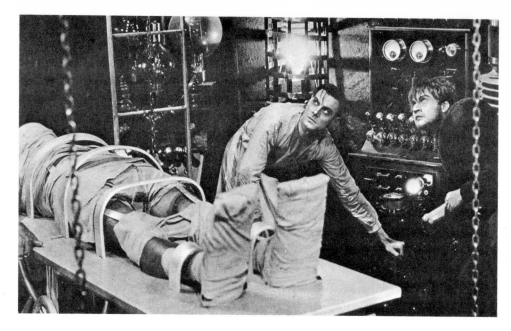

Mary Shelley's *Frankenstein* was brought to the screen by director James Whale. Here we see the expelled college student (Colin Clive) and his deformed assistant preparing to instill life in the motionless form on the laboratory table. (THE BETTMANN ARCHIVE, INC.)

The confused monster plays a tragic game with an innocent child in this famous sequence from *Frankenstein*. Interestingly, British censors allowed this scene to be shown, but not the killing of the hunchback.

(THE BETTMANN ARCHIVE, INC.)

Director James Whale gets sympathy for Frankenstein's monster (Boris Karloff) by showing how the creature was tormented during the first days of his life. The monster later breaks loose and hangs the vicious hunchback (Dwight Frye). Note the artificial setting in this original 1931 *Frankenstein* film.   (THE BETTMANN ARCHIVE, INC.)

In this climactic shot from *The Bride of Frankenstein*, the baron (Colin Clive) helps the terrifying but stunned bride (Elsa Lanchester) as her pathetic bridegroom (Boris Karloff) and Dr. Pretorious (Ernest Thesiger), watch.   (THE BETTMANN ARCHIVE, INC.)

Peter Lorre as the demented child-murderer in *M* (1931).
(HERMAN G. WEINBERG COLLECTION)

The classic shot of the great King Kong on top of the Empire State Building.   (HERMAN G. WEINBERG COLLECTION)

(*left*) In a scene from *King Kong*, Ann (Fay Wray) is placed in a tree so that Kong can protect her from the prehistoric animals he will have to destroy before beauty and beast will be safe in the giant ape's mountain retreat. Note the slight difference between foreground where the girl is and the transparency screen in the background.

(BETTMANN/SPRINGER FILM ARCHIVE)

TRADITION

Much of the traditional story has already been told about the motion picture industry's famous theatrical and literary monsters, vampires, mummies and mad scientists. Starting in the mid-thirties, studio after studio began the senseless ritual of resurrecting popular screen ghouls just to take advantage of an unsuspecting audience's fascination with terror. Thus films such as *Dracula's Daughter* (1936) and *Son of Frankenstein* (1939) relied more on the memory of things past than on the directors' talent which was too often lacking in this period. Except for some occasional outstanding screen performances by Charles Laughton in the 1939 movie *The Hunchback of Notre Dame* and Claude Rains in the 1941 remake of *The Phantom of the Opera,* the terror film seemed destined for oblivion. Most of the mythical movie kings had been established, many of the horror conventions cemented, and the majority of screen artists stereotyped for the next two decades. What remains now is for us to consider the exceptions to the cheap imitations that debased the terrors of the screen since the thirties, while at the same time offering some reasons why, beginning in the fifties and carrying through to the present, terror films have suddenly reappeared as a regular feature in movie theaters around the world.

Once again we need to fix our attention on Universal Studios, for it was here that the last fabulous film monster of legendary origins appeared in 1940: the werewolf. Interestingly enough, supernatural tales about men—"were"—who became wolves abound in the folklore of nations since the beginning of time, second in popularity only to the legendary vampires. Yet movies about lycanthropes (werewolves) did not gain any cinematic prominence until Universal's 1935 production, *The Werewolf of London*. Despite the celluloid emphasis on a gentle physician who, after being bitten by a werewolf, cannot escape being transformed into a savage beast, few film-goers failed to recognize that the new terror monster was none other than our old friend, Mr. Hyde. Thinking that the wolfman theme was doomed to failure, the studio heads cancelled any plans for sequels. By the end of the thirties, however, audiences were becoming increasingly restless with the feeble children of Kong, Dracula and Frankenstein. So the money men at Universal decided to try once more, only this time they wanted a novel approach to their story of a fiendish but pathetic creature.

Two elements were central to the possible success of the movie: a convincing plot and a competent cast. Curt Siodmak, the ill-used and much underrated writer-director, was assigned the screen-writing chores for *The Wolf Man*. (Seven years later he would also prepare the script for the fascinating motion picture *The Beast with Five Fingers*.) Unlike his predecessors in this field, Siodmak had no major literary source to adapt for his significant undertaking. But this worked to his advantage. Being forced to select judiciously and edit a host of superstitions and legends concerning werewolves, he was able to create a new and imaginative interpretation of a unique monster, the basic features of his plot remaining as the pattern for most future wolfman films. Few viewers of the day will ever forget the opening shot where the ominous quotation flashed on the screen:

Even a man who is pure in heart
And says his prayers by night,
Can become a wolf when the wolfbane blooms
And the autumn moon is bright.

Fade in to the joyful return of Lawrence Talbot, a carefree college student, to his Balkan home. Being university educated, Larry discounts many of the superstitions of his birthplace, particularly those rumors circulated by the frightened villagers who fear that a travelling gypsy caravan brings with it the curse of the werewolf. Then, one night, during a moonlight walk in the mysterious Transylvania woods, Lawrence Talbot, in the process of rescuing a woman being savagely attacked by a strange beast, receives a tragic neck bite. Terrible events follow that fateful evening. Larry, unable to account for the fantastic "dreams" he has had in connection with several recent unsolved killings, finally, in desperation, seeks the advice of the withered gypsy fortune-teller. It is she who reveals the horrible truth about that strange moonlit evening when her son, a werewolf, gave Talbot the curse of lyncanthropy. She shows him proof: the mark of the pentagram, the five-pointed star which appeared on his body following Larry's first murder and which will remain with him until he is killed either by a silver bullet or some other silver object.

Even more disturbing to the tormented man, he will be able to see the mark of the pentagram in the palms of his future victims. And so the young Talbot, frustrated in his attempts to convince any responsible person of his dilemma, lives in constant dread of the coming of the full moon and the blooming of the wolfbane. Mercifully, the end comes when under the spell of the curse Talbot is killed by his own father, who clubs the werewolf to death with the silver cane that Larry had insisted he carry.

The Wolf Man was an instant success in 1941. Besides the story's fresh appeal, the convincing camera work of Jack Valentine and the impressive make-up job of Jack Pierce, the cast distinguished itself with several memorable performances, particularly the superb Marie Ouspenskaya as the gypsy fortune-teller, Bela Lugosi as her werewolf son, and Claude Rains as the elder Talbot. But best of all was Lon Chaney Jr.'s portrayal of Lawrence Talbot.

In many respects, the wolfman role was not a good break for Creighton Chaney, whom Universal had hired more for his father's famous name than for his screen talents. Chaney had switched from the stage to the screen in 1932, shortly after his father's death, and had developed his talents to the point where in 1939 he gave to the movies one of its finest moments as he brilliantly played the poor, mindless drifter Lennie in *Of Mice and Men*. Only once more, in 1952, as the retired and aged sheriff in *High Noon* did Chaney reveal the wasted art he possessed. But after *The Wolf Man*, Chaney chose, for reasons best known to himself, to perform mechanically and monotonously over the next twenty years in exploitation films such as *The Ghost of Frankenstein, Frankenstein Meets the Wolfman, The Son of Dracula, The Mummy's Ghost, The Mummy's Curse, House of Dracula*, and *The House of Frankenstein*. When these relatively cheap, crude movies failed to attract audiences, he joined with Bud Abbott and Lou Costello in spoofing the very roles he had helped to downgrade: *Abbott and Costello Meet Frankenstein*, one of the famous forerunners of television's popular monster satires, *The Adams Family* and *The Munsters*. After that it is kinder to ignore the misguided and misdirected actor who never reached for better things.

In 1940, Paramount Pictures successfully exploited many of the techniques used by O'Brien and Schoedsack in *King Kong*, an approach employed years later by the creators of television's *Land of the Giants*. This time the film was *Dr. Cyclops* which told the story of the bald, bespectacled and mustached Dr. Alexander Thorkel who, living alone in the forbidden regions of the Amazon, experimented with mysterious rays which had the power to reduce men to doll-like size. Ellsworth Hoagland's extraordinary Technicolor photography enhanced the mood in the special effects scenes where, for example, Thorkel holds one of the little people in his giant hand (quite similar in style to Fay Wray being held by Kong) and then proceeds sadistically to smother the helpless human with a horrendous wad of cotton that has been dipped in ether. In addition, there were a series of death-defying encounters with giant insects and animals. Although Schoedsack's direction lacked distinction, Albert Dekker, one of the cinema's better character actors, made a successful transition from stage to screen, debuting as the sinister and strange scientist who tampered with powers generally denied mortal men.

The idea of shrinking people continued to fascinate screen terrorists, and a decade later director Jack Arnold in Universal-International's first-rate terror film *The Incredible Shrinking Man* demonstrated the rich potential of the theme. In this movie, a vacationing man accidentally comes in contact with a radioactive dust cloud, and from that point on begins to shrink until, at the film's conclusion, he is a minute speck looking up at the stars. The director and his staff, dealing with the plight of an individual against forces beyond the skill of science, showed just how epic such a film could be. While many of the sets and situations were reminiscent of *Dr. Cyclops,* the suspenseful build up and the uncompromising conclusion established a new high for this special brand of terror. Since then we have had people growing and shrinking with amazing frequency in motion pictures and television, the most famous example in recent years being Richard Fleischer's 1966 film *Fantastic Voyage,* where special effects photography more than compensates for the unbelievably trite and weak script.

Schoedsack and O'Brien made just one last attempt to improve their skill with adventure and monster films with *Mighty Joe Young*, which earned Willis O'Brien an Academy Award for special effects. It is this rather uninteresting film about a giant ape who is gentle and trainable which probably provided the basis for the television cartoon series *King Kong*. It is also this film which provided training for Ray Harryhausen, the current master of special effects photography. Unfortunately the monster movies that Harryhausen had developed for Universal, particularly the imaginative 1954 terror film *The Creature from the Black Lagoon*, did not catch on, although the artist's technical virtuosity was evident in a number of superb touches.

But if exploitation and exhaustion are the trademarks of the forties, there was at least one film artist who rose above the sterile imagination of Hollywood's movie-makers: Val Lewton. In many respects he synthesized the traditions and talents of filmdom's great terrorists. His particular macabre school of movie-making stressed the importance of suggestion and implication. Having come to the cinema with a heavy literary background and as a screenwriter for David Selznick, Lewton appreciated the traditional importance of a suspenseful, unnerving buildup, the priceless gift of being able to stimulate an audience's active imagination by a carefully constructed plot skillfully captured on celluloid. Furthermore, Lewton, like the great German masters who preceded him, possessed a rare gift which enabled him to sustain the mood of a film by using remarkably composed shots that were carefully edited.

His major opportunity came in 1942, when RKO studios decided to follow the practices of many of its competitors and make low-budget terror films, movies that capitalized on such economic shortcuts as using existing sets, inexpensive performers and temporarily unassigned technicians. To Lewton went the responsibility of making these "quickie" motion pictures. No one expected anything worthwhile by way of art. The studio's emphasis was definitely on making some easy money. But Lewton was not of that breed.

Probably the first thing that the creative producer-director did was hypothesize on how his "B" picture operation could rise above the limited expectations of his Hollywood environment. Believing as he did that the dread of the unknown was more frightening than any actual experience could be, Lewton mused over the fantastic virtues of the screen: clever sound effects, haunting shadows, menacing silences, dramatic irony, and most important of all, the camera's ability to control the viewer's experiences. Why not, he speculated, concentrate on manipulating the audience's fears rather than on emphasizing the shocking and violent confrontations?

The stage was set in 1942 to put his terrors to the test. Working with an imaginative script by DeWitt Bodeen and helped by the competent directing abilities of Jacques Tourneur, Lewton masterminded the splendid movie *The Cat People*. The plot concerned a frightened career woman, Irena, who was obsessed with the idea that she had inherited the dreadful curse of her Balkan ancestry: anger changes one into a deadly panther. She tries to postpone her marriage to Oliver Reed, telling him of her fears for the future, but he refuses to believe such nonsense about curses and beasts. The wedding takes place, but the couple remain very much apart in their attitudes, and Reed decides to seek psychiatric help for his bride. He also confides to his friend Alice some of his marital problems. When Irena discovers her husband's activities, particularly his relationship with another woman, she becomes incensed. Shortly thereafter, Alice has the first of several mysterious and frightening brushes with a strange creature that seems intent on murdering her. By now Irena is losing control of her sanity and goes to the psychiatrist for help. The misguided physician decides to prove how normal his patient is by making romantic advances to her. Irena, in turn, shows him just how inaccurate his diagnosis is by clawing him to death. In the struggle, however, she receives a fatal wound which allows her to live only long enough to reach the panther cage in the city zoo where she dies near the beasts she so resembled.

What made *The Cat People* such a remarkable movie, in addition to the fact it was so far superior to anything else being made at the time, was the absence of so many of the hackneyed visual encounters between the pursuer and the pursued. Instead, Lewton emphasized the fragile and unsuspecting moments of life which allow evil and danger to triumph. Even more fascinating was his reluctance to rely on shock values. For example, we never see Irena actually change from woman to beast. In almost every instance, Lewton achieves his terrifying effects by suggesting the shadowy, eerie presence of a menacing creature as Alice walks home, alone, unaware of her dangerous situation on a deserted street or in the lonely Central Park. The terror builds as she becomes uncomfortable, suspicious and finally frantic. The audience is made to empathize with the panic-stricken woman who sees ominous shadows, hears strange noises, and thinks incredible thoughts.

During the next five years, the clever Lewton developed his terror formula further, and film-goers everywhere were delighted by such unusual and entertaining horror tales as *I Walked with a Zombie, The Leopard Man, The Seventh Victim, The Curse of the Cat People, The Body Snatchers,* and *Bedlam.* In particular, the last two pictures, starring the great Karloff, were an indication of just how much Lewton had progressed in importance and freedom from limited budgets. Unfortunately, a heart attack finished Val Lewton in 1951, a very gifted artist who at 46 still had so much more to offer the world on film.

The only other rare exception to the decline in the art of the terror film in the forties took place in Europe, in the imaginative work of the brilliant Carl Dreyer. His cinematic fascination in 1943 turned to witchcraft, an area relatively unexplored in the macabre sphere of the screen. Only once before, in 1920, had a significant movie been made on the subject: *Witchcraft Through the Ages* (*Häxan*). In that film, Benjamin Christen, also a Scandinavian director, created a clinical, pseudo-documentary movie about pagan rituals down through the ages and up to the twentieth century. Because some of the shots, scenes and sequences were so vivid and explicit about the diabolical orgies of mankind, the movie was highly controversial and may have discouraged many film-makers trying to make a sequel, or even from venturing into the discussion again. Whatever the reasons, for almost twenty years after, most witches and voodoo ladies were relegated to jungle terror and to mysterious island melodramas. But during World War II, Dreyer decided to reopen the subject.

Instead of fixing his camera on the sensational and the sensuous, however, the ingenious artist magnificently turned his lens on capturing the psychological conflict of a spirited woman revolting against the traditions and hypocrisy of her society. *Days of Wrath* (*Vredens Dag*) focused on the isolated, small seventeenth-century Danish village where a stern, middle-aged Pastor Absalon imprisons, tortures and presides at the burning of an elderly woman convicted of witchcraft. From the flaming pyre and with her dying breath she curses her persecutor. Not long afterwards, the Pastor's second wife, young and hotblooded, finds herself being helplessly drawn into a love affair with her stepson Martin. Increasingly hostile to the pastor, Anne, in a moment of fury, reveals her relationship with Martin and angrily wishes that her husband were dead. With that, the Pastor suddenly suffers a fatal stroke. At her husband's funeral, Anne's mother-in-law, a vindictive and hateful individual, accuses the widow of being a witch. Abandoned by Martin and disgusted with the world in which she finds herself, Anne, too proud to defend herself, acknowledges that if this is what being a witch means, she is one of Satan's followers.

Dreyer's greatness, superbly demonstrated in *Day of Wrath,* was his arrangement and execution of individual shots, each one beautifully building into exquisite sequences. And within each shot, the master, using dramatic tonal shades of black and white, underscored how his visual images of a corrupt village were relevant for all men and all times.

Since Dreyer's film, witches have increased in popularity as film subjects, mostly notably as comic figures in movies like *Topper* or *Bell, Book and Candle,* and most recently as central characters in a highly successful television situation comedy, *Bewitched.* But that is not to say that there have not been some excellent treatments of the horrific sides of the witch story, particularly in such well-done dramatic and literary screen translations as *The Witches of Salem,* a French version of Arthur Miller's *The Crucible;* and *The Innocents,* England's adaptation of Henry James' novella *The Turn of the Screw.* But no motion picture in recent years has been as controversial or aesthetically pleasing as Polish director Roman Polanski's first American movie *Rosemary's Baby.*

Polanski is one of those exceptional people in the movie industry who not only knows what he's doing but enjoys doing it. Although relatively young—he was born in 1933—and new to the cinema—he finished his first short in 1958 and his first full-length movie in 1961—his three previous terror films showed genuine talent. In particular, his second feature *Repulsion,* to some degree, foreshadowed his work in *Rosemary's Baby.* The former showed the internal decay of an individual's mind as she senselessly and violently murders two individuals. In the latter, Polanski continued his macabre interest in shock and violence. As the director himself explains his methods, "It excites me to shock. I like to shock bourgeois audiences who cannot accept that other people may be different from them." And so in 1967, "the little giant" came to New York City to make a shocking terror film about pregnancy.

His motion picture follows the plot of Ira Levin's best-selling novel faithfully. The setting is the Dakota Apartment House on Central Park West where a young, childless couple come to live, the unfortunate wife continually asking her husband to agree to their having a child. He, in turn, refuses, arguing that they're not ready for a family. Then they meet their next-door neighbors, an elderly, busybody couple who share the wife's longing for a baby. Just one thing though: these older folks are practicing witches and they are eager that Satan father Rosemary's child. What follows as the ambitious husband agrees to sell his soul and his child to Satan's legions is a fascinating mixture of humor and horror, ending in the weird birth of an unseen child and a mother's faith that goodness can triumph over evil. But then again, that may not be it at all. The whole incident could be a dream, Rosemary's nightmare brought on by some hallucinations connected with pregnancy. Polanski himself claims that before and during the filming itself, he was extremely concerned with dreams, their temporal qualities and their realistic impact on the mind.

Cinematically conceived and effectively executed, the film, released in 1968, is also extremely well-cast. Mia Farrow gives an exciting performance as a lovely but ill-fated mother, John Cassavetes is very effective as one skunk of a husband, but the raves go to Ruth Gordon's delightful characterization of the chatty fiend who works tirelessly to bring Lucifer's earthly son into the world. Indeed so good is Miss Gordon's performance that in 1968 she became the first actress in the history of terror films to win an academy award as a supporting star.

If Polanski's work is unusual and skillful, if he succeeds as an expert in audience manipulation, it may be because of a conscious or subconscious debt to one of the master craftsmen of suspense: Alfred Hitchcock. Although this genius of the cinema has avoided any preoccupation with terror films, with the possible exception of *Psycho* and *The Birds*, it is almost impossible to view his movies without witnessing a murder or the revolting antics of some unbalanced mind. And what makes the viewing of such horrible moments so exciting and intriguing is Hitchcock's magnificent talent for creating, controlling, and sustaining tension and suspense.

In 1960, the witty director made what many film historians consider his first and best horror movie *Psycho*. In some respects similar to Lang's *M* and related in a sort of reverse situation to Polanski's *Repulsion* and *Rosemary's Baby*, Joseph Stefano's screenplay dealt with a madman's uncontrolled passion. For almost the first half hour of the movie, Hitchcock, anticipating the audience's expectations and emotions, leads his viewers astray by emphasizing the lonely and sad mid-afternoon flight of a beautiful woman who is stealing company funds. Later that night, exhausted, Marion finds shelter in a murky-looking motel, run by an outwardly pleasant young man who also takes care of his sickly mother residing in the adjoining, delapidated Victorian house.

Thanking Norman Bates for his interest in her comfort, Marion goes to her room and decides to take a shower before retiring. Then in the grandest tradition of shock, violence and terror, Norman's "mother" pulls back the shower curtain and unmercifully stabs Marion to death. Norman himself soon appears to clean up the bloody mess and dispose of the body, the clothes, and the car in nearby quicksand.

But Marion is missed, and the first of several inquiries begins with the appearance of Arbogast, an insurance detective who, hired to retrieve the stolen money, has traced Marion's escape to the Bates Motel. Almost immediately he becomes curious about old Mrs. Bates herself. He just about makes his way to the last step of the top floor of the ancient mansion before his curiosity gets him killed, again by the knife-wielding "mother." Fortunately his preliminary investigation has not been in vain. Just prior to entering the house, he had relayed by telephone his suspicions about the Bateses to Marion's lover and her sister.

Having learned from the local police authorities that

Norman's mother had died almost eight years ago, Lila and Sam converge on the sinister mansion and begin an intensive search of the rooms. It is Lila who first enters the basement where the dead body of Mrs. Bates is kept and comes face to face with the schizophrenic Norman who has been alternating between being his mother and himself. Just before Norman can commit another murder, Sam disarms him and the film closes with the homicidal maniac pensively sitting alone on a prison bench trying to justify his actions.

Although Hitchcock claimed that he was not trying in *Psycho* "to reconstruct an old-fashioned Universal horror-picture atmosphere," there is much in the film that is reminiscent of the old-fashioned "haunted house" movies going back to the early 1900's. Then, too, audiences had grown accustomed to their villains being obviously evil-looking and to their stars somehow surviving the most disastrous of plots. Thus, it is not altogether accidental that Janet Leigh, the most famous actress in the film, plays Marion, and that the pleasant, handsome Anthony Perkins murders her before one-third of the movie is over. It is precisely such examples of Hitchcock's manipulated editing and carefully controlled production methods that may have suggested to Polanski how the worst in people might be manipulated to make for the best screen terror.

The Polish director may have had one other expert teacher in the manipulative art of exploiting an audience's terror of the unknown: Henri-Georges Clouzot. This controversial and often unfairly maligned French director who came to the cinema first as film cutter and then spent ten years as a script writer and assistant director, at one time was accused, without any justification, of being a Nazi collaborator, and then was exiled from movies for a brief period. At another time, illness forced him into a sanitarium, interrupting his screen career for almost five years. But by 1955, he was an established director and Clouzot decided to experiment with terrorizing suspense and deliberate audience manipulation.

In some respects, like Hitchcock, the Frenchman claimed it was not his intention in *Diabolique* to dwell on the old horror-school tradition. Instead he wanted to delight himself "and the little child who sleeps in our hearts—the child who hides her head under the bed covers and begs, 'Daddy, Daddy, frighten me.'" If that was his intention, he certainly succeeded in terrorizing children of all ages everywhere his movie was shown.

In *Diabolique* the skillful director quickly establishes the mood, tensions and major characters in his expertly filmed opening sequences where the incompetent and brutal director of a seedy, provincial boys' school antagonizes one of his teachers, Nicole—also his mistress—once too often. Nicole then conspires with Michel's sickly wife, Christina, to murder him. Both women, having suffered considerably at the man's hands, agree that Michel is a sadist and must be done away with if they are to have any kind of life at all. A plan is devised and then put into operation, the end result being Michel's death and the subsequent throwing of his corpse into the school swimming pool. It would appear as if all had gone well. That is until a series of strange events occur: one of the children reports that he has seen the missing headmaster, the body mysteriously disappears from the pool, and the laundry returns the cleaned and pressed suit Michel was wearing the night he was murdered. Up to this point, Clouzot is superb. Like all the distinguished masters of terror, he has used the plausible, the possible to suggest, to imply the horror and fear that results from the unexplainable. But the film's conclusion, difficult to believe, demonstrates that Michel is not really dead after all. The entire terrifying affair, fiendishly designed by Nicole and Michel, has been for the sole purpose of giving Christina a fatal heart attack and allowing the husband to inherit the dead woman's estate.

If the art of Lewton and Dryer has somehow been passed along to directors like Clouzot, Hitchcock and Polanski, then it illustrates among other possibilities, that the visual techniques of terror are today understood by a relatively small number of artists. Except for such creative and original television work done in William Frye's *Thriller,* Joseph Stefano's *Outer Limits* and Rod Serling's *The Twilight Zone,* the terror film of the past seems on its last reel. This was foreshadowed in the forties.

But a new kind of macabre school of movie-making has taken its place, one that emphasizes sex, violence and shock above anything else. The question is, Why? How did it start? The answer to these questions may well be found by returning to Dr. Kracauer's thesis: motion pictures are related to society's stresses. Emerging from the horror of World War II, millions of people became increasingly terrified over the dangers of atomic radiation and a nuclear holocaust, the dehumanizing power of mass technology, and the uncertainty of interplanetary exploration. The movie industry was quick to realize that the world's fears provided an excellent new source for screen terrorists.

The fifties, therefore, saw a renaissance in macabre movies in which science-fiction and horror were unevenly mixed. From the four corners of the globe came coarse, crude moving pictures exploiting a frightened public's sensible realization that atomic power, uncontrolled and in the wrong hands, could destroy mankind. Some film-makers, as a result, specialized in presenting Stone Age creatures who were freed once more to terrorize mortals, their freedom being one of the unforeseen side effects of atomic testing. The more popular films of this category came not only from Universal-International studios but also from Japan's Eros where a flood of Godzilla movies were produced—Godzilla being a mutation sired by a prehistoric dinosaur and an easily forgettable relative of Kong.

Other studios took sadistic pleasure in pointing to the harmful side effects of radiation when tiny and controllable insects could suddenly be transformed into giant beasts intent on the shocking destruction of anyone and everyone, witnessed in isolated and vulnerable test sites in the United States when mammoth ants and terrifying spiders appeared. These movies may not have been very well-conceived, but every now and then you got your daily dose of shock.

Space travel, too, offered an excellent opportunity for screen terror. Not since the Flash Gordon and Buck Rogers serials of the thirties had film audiences witnessed so many imaginative gadgets, ingenious horror and splended entertainment. Creative artists like George Pal in his pioneering *Destination Moon* (1950) skillfully combined the superstitions of the age with the cinematic traditions of the past: animation, scaled models and live action were marvelously combined into new, fresh and terrifying moments of adventure and exploration. Probably the best example of the period was Fred Wilcox's excellent *Forbidden Planet* (1956), based upon Shakespeare's classic *The Tempest*. In this modern version, the mad scientist and his incredibly dangerous subconscious raise science-fiction terror to some very engrossing explorations of the strange and mysterious ways of man. But voyagers in space, we were reminded in the fifties, could come as well to our planet. And each of us who went to the movies then had a fond or frightening memory (or both) of some exciting film which showed Earth being invaded by Martians in flying saucers—*The War of the Worlds* (1953)—or a strange, deadly vegetable-like creature intent on killing human beings in *The Thing* (1951). Almost everyone in the movie audience soon began to think twice about unidentified flying objects and the role of science in world affairs.

With this new interest in the possible horrors of science and creatures from other worlds, movie-makers learned about a new generation's interest in shock and violence. It was this realization that led certain individuals to reconsider the visual treatments of the traditional terror films. For a brief time, certain producers experimented with 3-D movies, films which gave the impression that spears, knives and bodies were actually coming out of the screen toward the audience. But director André de Toth's 3-D remake of *House of Wax* (1953) proved little, except for foreshadowing Vincent Price's eventual rise to fame as a master of horror. The motion picture's many graphic gimmicks failed to impress anyone, and 3-D films went back to the drawing board.

But in 1957, a new producing unit in terror films emerged: Hammer Studios. This hitherto insignificant company decided that the Whale and Lewton tradition of movie-making was too mild for the present time, that relying on suggestion rather than on shock was passé. So they put some blood, eyeballs and sex into their up-dated version of the Shelley classic. *The Curse of Frankenstein* released in 1957, had little resemblance to anyone or anything in the past. No one connected with the production seemed concerned with developing suspense, establishing a mood, or allowing the audience to use its imagination. The focus was on revolting the viewer. The technique, helped by "living" color, emphasized detached limbs and eyeballs, half-robed women, and lots of violence. Just in case the censors objected, Hammer Studios released three versions ranging from a mild print of shocking scenes to a detailed, shot-by-shot account of the blood-letting sequences.

The film, the method and the subject matter appealed to the movie audiences of the day. Most important, the studio helped establish a new trend in terror films. They had clearly demonstrated that millions of people would pay just to be shocked by sadistic scenes of blood and torture. Furthermore, the film had given two new stars to the horror tradition: Peter Cushing and Christopher Lee.

In 1958, *The Horror of Dracula* was released. Although it too suffered from the over-emphasis on blatant shock and violence, the closing sequence where Van Helsing (Cushing) traps Dracula (Lee) is a visual masterpiece of a vampire's death. Since the Hammer Studios and its repertory company have put their bodies and violent spirits to work on injecting some blood and gore into the traditional terror kings of previous decades, and this accounts for such movies as *The Two Faces of Dr. Jekyll; The Phantom of the Opera; The Revenge of Frankenstein; The Evil of Frankenstein; The Curse of the Mummy's Tomb; Dracula, Prince of Darkness; Dracula has Risen from the Grave;* and *Frankenstein Must be Destroyed.*

Not to be outdone by the Englishmen, America's Roger Corman decided it was time to revive Edgar Allan Poe, only now the director would match the gifted writer's blood-curdling skills with some cinematic gore of his own. Beginning his major directing responsibilities in 1955, he first gained notoriety with his screen adaptation of Poe's *The Fall of the House of Usher.* Needless to say, whatever Hammer Studios can do, Corman can also do. In addition to the repulsive shots of violent confrontations and skin-piercing tortures, Corman has demonstrated an unusual gift for establishing authentic settings and providing believable motivations. He has been further blessed with a talented actor like Vincent Price who is one of the few stars that demonstrates the lost art of controlled terror and a welcome sense of humor, even in the most depressing moments of screen violence. Since the 1960 production of *The Fall of the House of Usher,* Corman has filmed such Poe classics as *The Pit and the Pendulum, The Premature Burial, The Tales of Terror* and *The Haunted Palace.*

The present state of affairs might best be summed up in the sixties' most successful science-fiction terror film: Franklin Schaffner's *The Planet of the Apes.* This 1968 movie synthesis of fantasy plots ranging from Shakespeare to O'Brien tells of a space journey which returns Astronaut Charlton Heston back to earth at some distant time in the future. And as the bitter and lonely voyager holds the broken pieces of the Statue of Liberty in his hands, he warns us of the madness of our age and the dangers we may yet face. He reminds us that man, in order to survive, must have the good sense to fear the unknown and to brave the unexpected.

Henry Hull as a werewolf in *The Werewolf of London.* John Barrymore and Fredric March used similar make-up to characterize Mr. Hyde.

(THE BETTMANN ARCHIVE, INC.)

In *The Wolf Man* (1941) Lon Chaney, Jr., used yak hair to create the terrifying werewolf we see here clutching the unconscious heroine (Evelyn Ankers). (BETTMANN/SPRINGER FILM ARCHIVE)

In this typical scene from *Dr. Cyclops*, the evil scientist (Albert Dekker) captures one of his tiny experiments (Charles Halton).

(BETTMANN/SPRINGER FILM ARCHIVE)

Grant Williams, shrinking due to a mysterious illness, is comforted when he meets midget April Kent, his own height, in *The Incredible Shrinking Man*. Notice how special props and a transparency screen are used to create the realistic effects. (BETTMANN/SPRINGER FILM ARCHIVE)

The pre-historic frog monster (Ricou Browning) comes up under the boat of the expedition seeking to capture it in this scene from *The Revenge of the Creature* (1955). (THE BETTMANN ARCHIVE, INC.)

Fantastic Voyage has a unique twist to terror. Men, having discovered how to reduce themselves to microbe size, send a team of experts inside a man's body to cure his illness. Here we see the voyagers outside their miniature craft exploring the inside of the patient's body.

(BETTMANN/SPRINGER FILM ARCHIVE)

In 1957, Hammer Studios put out a new version of Shelley's monster, *The Curse of Frankenstein*. Because Karloff's unique make-up was copyrighted by Universal, Christopher Lee (seen here) had to create a new appearance for himself.　(THE BETTMANN ARCHIVE, INC.)

The Cat People, with Irena (Simone Simon) brooding about her future life with her husband (Kent Smith). Note the way shadows are used to heighten the tension.　(THE BETTMANN ARCHIVE, INC.)

In this crucial moment from *Rosemary's Baby*, the terrified mother (Mia Farrow) approaches the crib of her new-born child to see whether she has given life to the devil's son. (BETTMANN/SPRINGER FILM ARCHIVE)

The granddaddy of all witchcraft films was this 1921 Swedish film, *Häxan* (*Witchcraft Through the Ages*). (HERMAN G. WEINBERG COLLECTION)

Norman (Anthony Perkins) has just cleaned up the bathroom after his first murder in *Psycho*. Hitchcock used a great deal of bird symbolism in the movie: the murderer takes an interest in taxidermy, and in almost every key scene there were pictures of birds or stuffed owls looking at Norman Bates, as if they could see him for what he was.

(BETTMANN/SPRINGER FILM ARCHIVE)

Vincent Price, the current king of terror, in *The Pit and the Pendulum* (1961). (CULVER PICTURES, INC.)

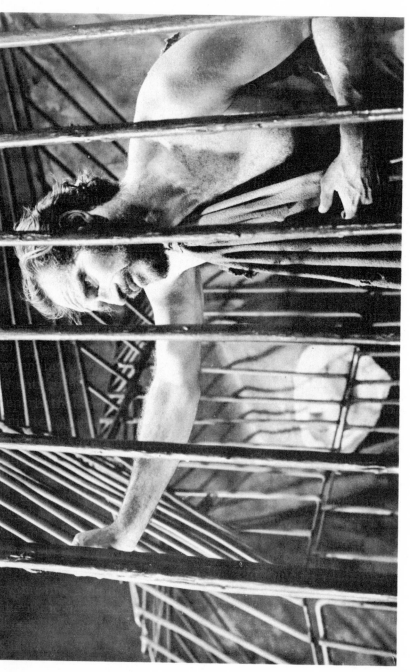

In *The Planet of the Apes*, Charlton Heston plays the role of a captured astronaut who has to convince his captors that man, as we know him, deserves to live.　(BETTMANN/SPRINGER FILM ARCHIVE)

REFLECTIONS

Before we leave the terrors of the screen, we might pause and consider what horror movies dwell upon and what special appeal they have for us today. We can readily agree that such motion pictures offer escape from our commonplace, everyday existence and further provide thrilling experiences that many of us consciously avoid in real life. Yet escape, entertainment and amusement are also characteristics of the other mass media as well. What then is so special about terror films?

No easy answer is readily available. For one thing, terror films appeal to our curiosity, to our unquenchable thirst to know more about the regions of the unknown where all of us, from crib to coffin, often consider exploring and then swiftly change our minds. The good Dr. Jekyll, for example, was curious about his new hidden evil self, those horrible and mysterious emotions which he felt existed in his innermost thoughts. So also is each of us interested in those unseen forces of darkness stored up within our breasts. But few among us would risk life, limb and fortune to find the answer. Certainly, Dr. Jekyll, with his unfortunate discovery, would warn us against it.

Second, terror films remind us of our ignorance and the compelling need for intelligent men to distinguish between superstition and truth, to investigate forbidden realms and not be frightened by the imagined terrors of the unknown. Thus three scholars searching for the answers to Egypt's marvelous past must confront an ancient pharaoh's curse if they dare open the coffin of Im-ho-tep. So too must Baron Victor Frankenstein face unimaginable horrors if he persists in his secret experiments to create life. The quest for knowledge, the search for creation remain timeless challenges, but how many of us draw back in terror, frightened to go beyond the acceptable borders of our experiences. Yet by watching terror films, we identify with the screen stars who boldly attack society's conventions, bravely defy the sacred taboos of bygone eras, and foolishly scoff at the startling dangers from the unknown. The performers' acts mirror our wishes. When disaster strikes, we thankfully are safe and secure in our seats, party to the voyage beyond the known without having to suffer the consequences.

Third, these films cater to those moods of our emotional lives that demand contact with the macabre and the supernatural, that take pleasure in viewing the hideous, grotesque and monstrous. We secretly derive pleasure from the fact that we are more fortunate than others, even though many of us feel guilty about such feelings. This is in no small part due to the values we place on success, competition and aggressiveness. Those who hunger for power at the expense of spiritual values have but to see the fate of Counts, Barons and scientists who populate many of the terror films. And which of us is not more satisfied with his lot in life after watching the misfortunes of a Jonathan Harker, or a Lawrence Talbot, two men who through no fault of their own came to know the terror that night can bring.

Our concern in this book, however, has not been terror for terror's sake, such as that found in poorly conceived and executed film melodramas where blood and gore serve only to mask the ineptness of the director's work. Rather, we have been interested in those rare motion pictures calculated to stimulate man's limitless imagination about himself and the world he inhabits—movies that visually illustrate the strange, unexpected and horrible turn of events which threaten our powers of reason.

What is most unique about terror films, therefore, is their ability to combine entertainment with education, shock with significant meaning, and horror with human feelings.

Looking back on those splendid films, each of us can recognize that time has placed new names among the honored list of the screen stars of horror and fear—new artists whose imagination and skill have changed the appearance of terror and taken it into hitherto forbidden areas. But neither the age nor the artists have eliminated the pressures of the present and the uncertainty of the future. Man is still man. And if he is to survive and move forward with any hope for success, man needs to fear, to worry about the dangers of the unseen, and to be reminded of his fragile existence in an unpredictable world.

So long as man suffers and reaches for better things, so long is the work of film artists only just begun.

BIBLIOGRAPHY

BIBLIOGRAPHY

The author believes that the following selective book list will help the curious reader in discovering more information about the terrors of the screen. Because of this book's length, many film artists were not adequately discussed, nor were individual writers acknowledged. Anyone consulting the following books which your author has found extremely useful will have no difficulty in deciding which works were made use of, what was taken from them, and where we each parted company.

Ackerman, Forrest J. *The Best From Famous Monsters of Filmland.* New York: Paperback Library, Inc., 1964.

Armes, Roy. *French Cinema Since 1946—Volume One: The Great Tradition.* Cranbury: A.S. Barnes & Co., 1966.

Balshofer, Fred J. and Arthur C. Miller. *One Reel A Week.* Berkeley: University of California Press, 1967.

Baxter, John. *Hollywood in the Thirties.* Cranbury: A.S. Barnes & Co., 1968.

Butler, Ivan. *The Horror Film.* Cranbury: A.S. Barnes & Co., 1967.

Clarens, Carlos. *An Illustrated History of the Horror Film.* New York: Capricorn Books, 1967.

Cowie, Peter. *Swedish Cinema.* Cranbury: A.S. Barnes & Co., 1966.

Crowther, Bosley. *The Great Films: Fifty Golden Years of Motion Pictures.* New York: G.P. Putnam's Sons, 1967.

Drake, Douglas. *Horror.* New York: Macmillan, 1966.

Everson, William K. *The Bad Guys: A Pictorial History of the Movie Villain*. New York: The Citadel Press, 1964.

Gifford, Denis. *Movie Monsters*. New York: E.P. Dutton and Co., Inc., 1969.

Gow, Gordon. *Suspense in the Cinema*. Cranbury: A.S. Barnes & Co., 1968.

Higham, Charles and Joel Greenberg. *Hollywood in the Forties*. Cranbury: A.S. Barnes & Co., 1968.

Jacobs, Lewis. *The Rise of the American Film: A Critical History*. New York: Teachers College, Columbia University, 1969.

Kael, Pauline. *Kiss Kiss Bang Bang*. Boston: Atlantic, Little, Brown and Company, 1968.

Knight, Arthur. *The Liveliest Art: A Panoramic History of the Movies*. New York: Macmillan, 1957.

Kracauer, Siegfried. *From Caligari to Hitler: A Psychological History of the German Film*. Princeton: Princeton University Press, 1947.

Lannig, Arthur, editor. *Classics of the Film*. Madison: Wisconsin Film Society Press, 1965.
————. *Film Notes*. Madison: Wisconsin Film Society Press, 1960.

Marlowe, Don. *The Hollywood That Was*. Fort Worth: Branch-Smith, Inc., 1969.

McBride, Joseph, editor. *Persistence of Vision: A Collection of Film Criticism*. Madison: The Wisconsin Film Society Press, 1968.

Meyers, Warren B. *Who is That?: The Late Late Viewers Guide to the Old Old Movie Players*. New York: Personality Posters, Inc., 1967.

Perry, George. *The Films of Alfred Hitchcock*. New York: Dutton, 1965.

Robinson, David. *Hollywood in the Twenties*. Cranbury: A.S. Barnes & Co., 1968.

Scheuer, Steven H., editor. *Movies on TV*. New York: Bantam Books, 1968.

Thomas, Bob. *Thalberg: Life and Legend*. New York: Doubleday, 1969.

Truffaut, Francois with the collaboration of Helen G. Scott. *Hitchcock*. New York: Simon & Schuster, 1967.

Tyler, Parker. *Classics of the Foreign Film: A Pictorial Treasury*. New York: Bonanza Books, 1962.

Wood, Robin. *Hitchcock's Films*. Cranbury: A.S. Barnes & Co., 1965.

INDEX

120

122